POSITION OF THE DAY
SEX FORTUNES
POSITIONS AND PREDICTIONS
FOR EVERY BIRTHDAY

 FROM NERVE.COM

CHRONICLE BOOKS
SAN FRANCISCO

Library of Congress Cataloging-in-Publication Data:
Position of the day : sex fortunes : positions and predictions for every
birthday / from Nerve.com.
p. cm.
ISBN 978-0-8118-5999-8
1. Sex—Miscellanea. 2. Sex—Humor. I. Nerve.com (Computer file) II. Title.

HQ25.P67 2008
306.702'07—dc22
2008010684

Manufactured in Canada
Designed by Erik Olsen Graphic Design
Written by Jennifer Prediger with contributions from Caitlin MacRae
Contributing Artists: Jason Walton and Eliza Stein

10 9 8 7 6 5 4 3 2 1

Chronicle Books LLC
680 Second Street
San Francisco, CA 94107
www.chroniclebooks.com

POSITION OF THE DAY
SEX FORTUNES

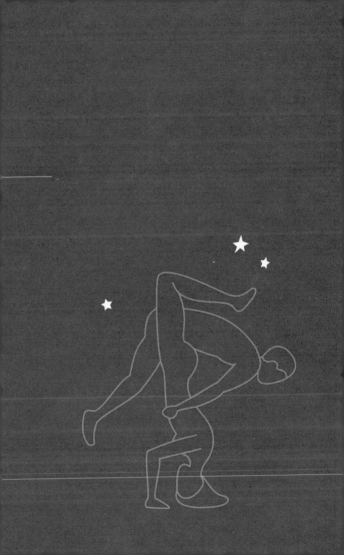

INTRODUCTION

What's Your Position?

Welcome to *Position of the Day: Sex Fortunes*. Offering positions and predictions for every birthday, sex fortunes are Nerve.com's new approach to making sure that everyone's birthday is a truly special day. We all know our astrological signs. It's about time we learned something just as important: our very own sex positions.

We spent many a raucous day and sleepless night working to bring you the best in inventive, crafty, and otherwise death-defying positions. The accompanying fortunes, painstakingly handcrafted to fit your birthday style, aren't just solid advice. They're an extra-special glimpse into your sexual presence—past, current, and future—that'll move you toward a more fantastic, fun, fortunate year of getting it on.

Whether you consult the book on special occasions or choose to treat every day like it's your birthday, we hope you'll get as much out of it as we put into it.

Now bring out that birthday suit and get to work.

—The Nerve Staff

THE POSITIONS

THE BALL DROP

COMPATIBLE BIRTHDAY ★ March_04

Always one for dramatic flair, your primary-school teachers placed
bets on whether you'd become a drama major or a drag queen.
You've always been game to don a costume (or a fellow named
Don). Your most popular costume? The one where you're dressed
as a gob knobbler.

THE SAN FRANCISCO TREAT

COMPATIBLE BIRTHDAY ★ December_11

Having read Joseph Campbell your sophomore year in college, you really took the idea of Joyous Participation to heart. Now you participate joyously whenever and wherever possible.

THE OPEN HEART

COMPATIBLE BIRTHDAY ★ May_30

You have always had an open heart—which brings much love, adventure, and joy into your world. Eat plenty of fish and omega-3s and this open-heart quality will come in handy 20 to 30 years from now. Some eating habits never go out of style.

THE MULTITASKING EXECUTIVE

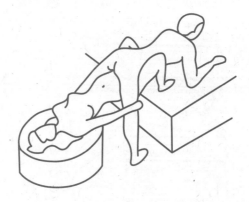

COMPATIBLE BIRTHDAY ★ June_02

There you are, cell phone in hand, shredding documents and banking online. You with your 70-hour work weeks and advanced-degree, Type-A personality have found a way to get it done while getting it done—raising your productivity (and reproductivity) levels to impressive heights.

THE FORTUITOUS FAINT

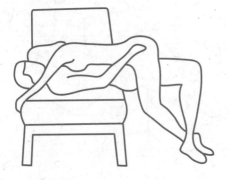

COMPATIBLE BIRTHDAY ★ August_22

Never one to be faint of heart, your low blood pressure has made you more faint of body. This has been both a curse and a blessing. An inopportune fainting spell nearly got you run over by a train. On the other hand, fainting came in handy that time you were getting mugged and the last time you saw your ex.

THE BENDABLE FEAST

COMPATIBLE BIRTHDAY ★ June_01

You are the kind of person who takes great pleasure in making soup for others. Your keen appetite nearly matches your desire to sate the appetite of those you care about. The only things that could stand in the way of gastronomical bliss are your occasional gastrointestinal issues.

THE THINKER

COMPATIBLE BIRTHDAY ★ September_24

Thoughtful and provocative, you enchant members of the opposite sex with your intellectual prowess. Your own gender is equally captivated by your athletic abilities. You are well read—and your vast knowledge is evident in your work. Though your focus is sometimes elsewhere, you always manage to take care of things.

THE "YOU MAY NOW KISS THE BRIDE"

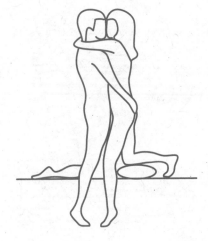

COMPATIBLE BIRTHDAY ★ April_05

When you first heard about a French kiss, you actually heard wrong. Though you have been told that what you're doing is more Polish, you've still let your original approach remain true—which has brought you much pleasure and fame in Paris and elsewhere.

THE BRUSH STROKE

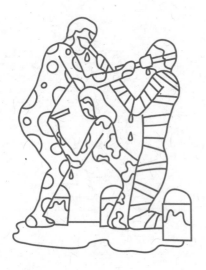

COMPATIBLE BIRTHDAY ★ July_31

You were once fired from a job as a house painter, which led you to become a graffiti artist instead. Your gift for desecrating homes, buildings, and the sides of buses has brought you notoriety and also a healthy amount of jail time—where you learned you also have a talent for being someone's bitch.

PUSH INS

COMPATIBLE BIRTHDAY ★ April_15

Your strength and coordination are most impressive (especially considering that you failed gym). Steady and steadfast, you hold firm until you achieve your goal. You are a late bloomer. When you peak later in life, you will help others make it to the mountaintop right beside you.

THE ACCORDION

COMPATIBLE BIRTHDAY ★ June_22

Polka may be your music of choice, but that doesn't keep you from approaching life like a squeezebox waiting for your signature touch. Given how good you are at pushing buttons, it's not surprising that you have people lined up to experience your special talents.

MAD HOT BALLROOM

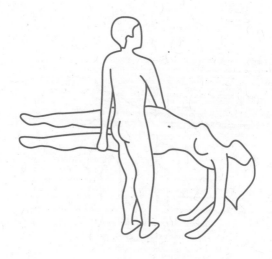

COMPATIBLE BIRTHDAY ★ June_13

You are a born leader—most fulfilled when taking matters into your own hands. Delighting in public performance, the world truly is your stage. You have a quick mind and often win trivia games. When the question "What do you do with a drunken sailor?" is asked, you always have a fresh new answer.

JANUARY_13

TWO CHAIR SNARE

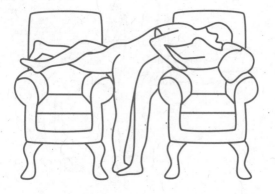

COMPATIBLE BIRTHDAY ★ November_05

You have a taste for fine things—and are not afraid to use them for your and others' enjoyment. No plastic-covered couch or "good china" for you. This is a wonderful and generous quality, but you might want to put a coaster under your drink once in a while.

THE HOT SEAT

COMPATIBLE BIRTHDAY ★ May_21

You are easy to please and find opportunities for pleasure where most others are content to just sit down. Your ingenuity is a benefit to all who know you. Your creative, spontaneous nature lends itself to boundless and extraordinary earthly delights.

THE "NOT SURE WE'RE DOING THIS RIGHT"

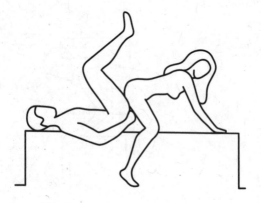

COMPATIBLE BIRTHDAY ★ March_15

The scientific method has never failed you, but sometimes it's not clear if your methodology is right. Keep up with your experimentation and you will likely be rewarded with a whopping grant—a Nobel Prize or at least a MacArthur Fellowship.

THE SIXTY-EIGHT

COMPATIBLE BIRTHDAY ★ March _14

You are a visionary, diving into things headfirst. Never one to put your own needs ahead of others', your work relations are deep and satisfying, and you are successful in almost all your undertakings.

"CAN I BUY YOU A DRINK?"

COMPATIBLE BIRTHDAY ★ June_20

Often thought of as shy, you've never let that get in the way of a loud climax. Even though Grandma always told you "Don't be shy," you quickly learned that's probably not what she had in mind.

THE VERY HANDY MAN

COMPATIBLE BIRTHDAY ★ May_14

You have everything a person could want, including the kitchen sink. But what good is all that stuff when most of it is broken? Take better care of your things. And if something is busted, you'll be well-served to call a capable handywoman or repairman.

JANUARY_19

THE HAPPY HOUR

COMPATIBLE BIRTHDAY ★ October_10

Drinking is both a vice for you and a powerful source of courage.
Keep tipping that glass and you will be certain to find the courage
to marry the wealthy man or woman of your dreams. You believe in
sharing your wealth and good fortune for the benefit of all. This is
toastworthy. Three cheers for you.

THE WHEN IN DOUBT

COMPATIBLE BIRTHDAY ★ April_28

When things fall through, you are the kind of person who has a Plan B at the ready—you always know what to do when all else fails. With your faith in your ability to come out on top, you've never been called a Doubting Thomas.

THE EXTRA POINT

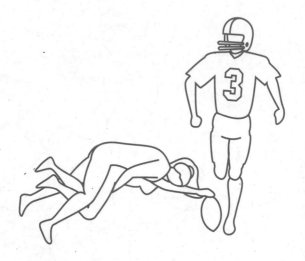

COMPATIBLE BIRTHDAY ★ July_11

You don't have to wait until game time to hike the balls. Try practicing even during the off-season. You know how to play the game. Some have even called you a player. Never mind that. Keep your eye on the prize. You'll go the distance and score big for everyone involved. Touchdown!

THE MOMA INSTALLATION

COMPATIBLE BIRTHDAY ★ September_19

You are capable of creating work worthy of competitive bidding prices at Sotheby's. Critics and collectors alike have much to say about your art. "Notable," "fresh," "new," and "daring" are things you are likely to hear often.

DEATH BECOMES HER

COMPATIBLE BIRTHDAY ★ August_08

While others are out drinking body shots, you, dear Aquarius, stay in gulping fish oil. When you belch it may smell like cod, but those whiskey dicks have nothing on your stamina.

THE QUEEN OF THE HILL

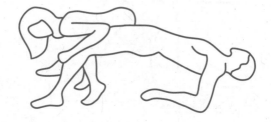

COMPATIBLE BIRTHDAY ★ May_24

You have always been the scrapple in the apple. The top of the heap. Whether dropped on an ant hill or Capitol Hill, you are sure to reign supreme. Use your crown wisely and with grace and be generous in sharing the family jewels.

JANUARY_25
THE OTTO-MAN

COMPATIBLE BIRTHDAY ★ August_06

Like an able mechanic, you've been called an auto woman or "The Otto-Man." You have no fear going under a greasy hood. You fix up even the most neglected vehicle, turning it into a well-oiled engine running on high-octane gasoline.

THE DOCTOR IS IN

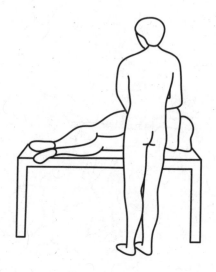

COMPATIBLE BIRTHDAY ★ October_05

Always wanting to make your mother proud, you are the type who will go the distance and become a doctor. As an internist, your bedside manner makes you the favored young physician during your residency. You have a bright future of HMOs ahead of you.

THE CLEANING SERVICE

COMPATIBLE BIRTHDAY ★ December_10

Obsessive-compulsive disorder is what gives your life order. Nary a hair on your bathroom sink or a dust bunny in a corner, you clean up in the extreme.

THE FRIENDLY ASSASSIN

COMPATIBLE BIRTHDAY ★ November_30

A friend in need is a friend indeed. You happen to be both. You are a taker and a giver. And likely a paid assassin—or an executor, if you will, always happy to carry out the will of others.

THE CATCH AND RELEASE

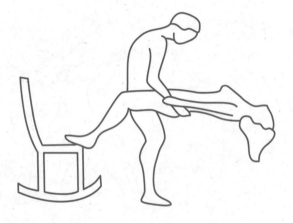

COMPATIBLE BIRTHDAY ★ June_19

A naturalist at heart, you've always taken inspiration from nature. A tender-hearted and able fisherman, you know how to reel them in, but always release your catch before the hooks get too deep.

THE INDECENT PROPOSAL

COMPATIBLE BIRTHDAY ★ July_23

You've always longed for commitment—the kind where you get down on one knee and live happily ever after—or at least for a few minutes. You will get your "I do" along with several "Oh, Gods."

BREAKFAST OF CHAMPIONS

COMPATIBLE BIRTHDAY ★ May_03

Some people like to dine at home. You have always enjoyed eating out. You have a few restaurants you frequent on a regular basis, and the waitresses love to see you because you're such a thoughtful customer and always leave such a big tip.

WAGGING THE DOG

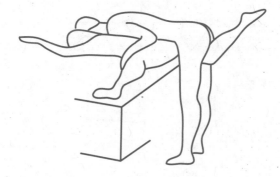

COMPATIBLE BIRTHDAY ★ July_04

You have always been one to enjoy a good old wives' tale. Even though your grandmother told you that having sex standing up was a form of contraception, you knew that to be a bunch of spunk bunk. But now you enjoy making new wives' tales all your own.

THE NUMBER 3

COMPATIBLE BIRTHDAY ★ May_10

Though your role model as a child was Little Miss Muffet, you never quite could figure out what a "tuffet" was. But you have sat upon many other fine things, and you have enjoyed every last bite of your "curds and whey."

SITTING ON THE DOCK OF THE BAY

COMPATIBLE BIRTHDAY ★ October_20

Those who know you would call you a bit cheeky. You always know when to insert a sly dig. And with a quick-witted tongue like yours, you always please those it comes into contact with.

THE ROCKING HORSE

COMPATIBLE BIRTHDAY ★ September_27

You don't mind backbreaking work if you can reap the benefits of it. Keep your health insurance premiums paid and keep going to those Pilates classes, and you will be greatly fulfilled.

THE LOST REMOTE

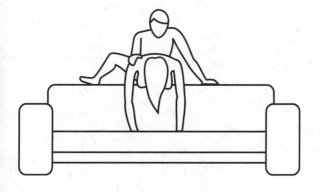

COMPATIBLE BIRTHDAY ★ December_29

With a definite knack for your field, you always get a big Christmas bonus due to your excellent sales record, and you like to blow your wad on fancy gadgets. But money can't buy a good memory, so you often need help figuring out where you stuck all those shiny new appliances.

THE BUNNY SLOPE

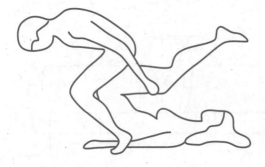

COMPATIBLE BIRTHDAY ★ July_08

When you have a crush on someone, it's not something to be taken lightly. Slow to be attracted, your interests pull both you and your intended together like a high-powered magnet. In all your romantic endeavors, make sure you have the right polarity or your strong forces may repel each other.

THE WAIT A MINUTE, MR. POSTMAN

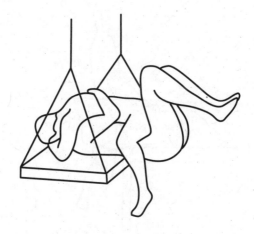

COMPATIBLE BIRTHDAY ★ November_06

You'd like to swing on a star and carry some of those moonbeams home in a jar. But you're actually better off just where you are. Just try not to fall from grace—or the swing.

"YOU HAVE THE RIGHT TO REMAIN SILENT"

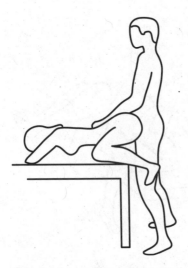

COMPATIBLE BIRTHDAY ★ September_17

Your mama always told you never to put your elbows on the table. But she never had what you're having. And that's too bad. She was a dull vegetarian who never partook of the cornucopia of tastes and delights you have opened yourself up to.

BILL AND TED'S EXCELLENT ADVENTURE

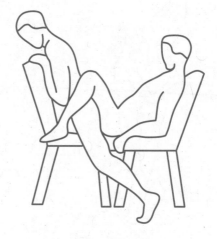

COMPATIBLE BIRTHDAY ★ June_28

As a member of elected office, you have moved quickly up the ranks to ranking chairman of an important House subcommittee. Your tenacity, determination, and loyalty to your office keep you serving your constituency. On Election Day, it's clear you've won their vote.

THE BREAST EXAM

COMPATIBLE BIRTHDAY ★ July_20

You know how to hang, and you hang with the best of them.
Nothing intimidates you. You may be afraid of heights, but you
manage to reach great peaks. Keep reaching high but always keep
your feet on the ground.

FIDDLER UNDER THE ROOF

COMPATIBLE BIRTHDAY ★ November_07

You care about the details, and because you pay such close attention, you are likely to find treasure wherever you look. You're the kind of person who spots a quarter on the ground on your way to catch a bus. Lucky pennies might as well have your name on them. (Keep in mind they are also frequently covered in urine as well.)

THE TEETER TROTTER

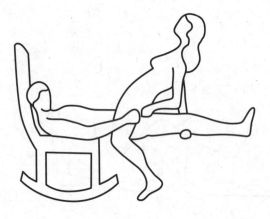

COMPATIBLE BIRTHDAY ★ March_11

As a child, you loved horses and excelled at all things equestrian.
Your birthday wish every year was for a pony, but you never got
one. Thankfully, you did have an excellent equine experience at
summer camp. This blissful memory is something that gives you joy
even when the horse and carriage of love and marriage is less than
you'd hoped for.

THE TOOTSIE ROLL

COMPATIBLE BIRTHDAY ★ June_24

Your knack for building things has brought you in close contact with tools and machinery—jackhammers and steamrollers in particular. Keep on paving the way, and your road will be smooth up ahead.

CUPID'S ARROW

COMPATIBLE BIRTHDAY ★ May_11

You don't want anything to do with a lover who doesn't want you.
Unfortunately for you, this is about 98 percent of the population.
Thank goodness for the intervention of spells, hexes, and the gods.
They are your only hope.

THE BEST IN SHOW

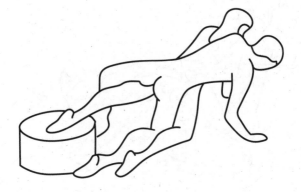

COMPATIBLE BIRTHDAY ★ June_16

You have been told on more than one occasion that you look like a Matisse. Not the long in the face kind, but the dancing naked in a circle kind. Your life is one good spin around the Maypole.

THE OLD AND THE RESTLESS

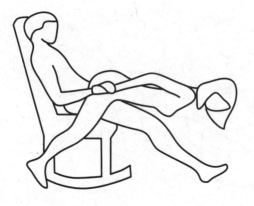

COMPATIBLE BIRTHDAY ★ December_14

You're young enough to know that rocking chairs aren't just for sipping mint juleps. You follow your own destiny, even if it takes you in an unusual direction. You eat pancake sandwiches for lunch and tap dance to celebrate the sunset. And you're never out of line.

THE RUNNING WITH SCISSORS

COMPATIBLE BIRTHDAY ★ April_23

By cutting a big swath through your admirers, you make quite an impact on people. You also get points for putting style before comfort. You are fashionating.

THE STAND AND DELIVER

COMPATIBLE BIRTHDAY ★ October_27

If you are ever to enjoy your life, now is the time. Face things head-on and be present for the greatness right before your very eyes. You are in a unique position to pause and enjoy exactly where you are—even if you are being held for ransom.

THE "D'OH"

COMPATIBLE BIRTHDAY ★ August_12

You are on the verge of a major breakthrough in your life. The wall holding you back will soon come crumbling down, so brace yourself. You don't want to hit the floor along with the plaster.

THE EM-IN-EM

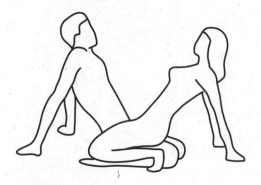

COMPATIBLE BIRTHDAY ★ March_12

When you were a kid your talent for games was discovered. Boggle, Hungry Hippos, Uno—you crushed all opponents. Then in college you took up yoga and discovered that with a little effort you could also really excel at Twister. You have held multiple titles in the field ever since.

THE TO EACH HIS OWN

COMPATIBLE BIRTHDAY ★ July_29

There is no need to bear the weight of the world on your shoulders.
Share your burdens—distributing the weight will free you up creatively
to do things you never even knew were possible—like drinking apple
cider upside down.

THE "GIVE ME AN A"

COMPATIBLE BIRTHDAY ★ January_15

Add a little "one-two, cha-cha-cha" to your routine by taking dance lessons. But choose your dance partners well. If you lead, you need someone who can follow. Be careful not to step on any toes.

THE NIGHT IN

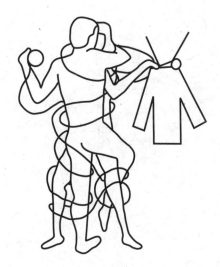

COMPATIBLE BIRTHDAY ★ May_15

Sit back and relax and take in the beauty around you. Your opportunities for relaxation are expanding. It is time for you to enjoy what is in front of you and what is behind you. Your hard work has brought you to this very fortunate position.

THE MARDI GRAB

COMPATIBLE BIRTHDAY ★ December_27

Baubles and bangles and beads are the stuff every lady (or gentleman)
loves. And every lady (or gentleman) loves you—even if she/he has
trouble looking beyond your mask.

THE SERVING SPOON

COMPATIBLE BIRTHDAY ★ July_18

You have your hands in some pretty exciting projects these days.
Don't get overwhelmed by the tasks at hand. You are more than well
equipped to do the job. Keep your focus and you will reach great
depths.

SO THEY ALL ROLLED OVER . . .

COMPATIBLE BIRTHDAY ★ September_22

Some people like to sit and watch the grass grow. Not you. You like to stare up at the clouds and see a circus of puffy white animals, race cars, philosophers, and rock stars float by. This fulfills you deeply and feeds your healthy imagination, driving you to profound creative acts.

THE LOCK 'N' LOAD

COMPATIBLE BIRTHDAY ★ August_16

Your creative force is like a coiled spring, ready to explode outward. Find new ways to connect with what inspires you. Take pictures. Write stories. Test out your drawing skills. Then post it all on the Internet. The results will be lucrative.

THE BREAK A LEG

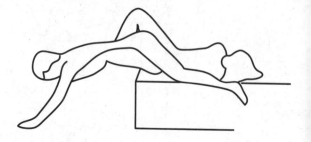

COMPATIBLE BIRTHDAY ★ March_17

You know how to keep a leg up on the competition. Your master's degree in business administration will take you to the top levels of Fortune 100 companies. Your innovation in the boardroom will bring you many stock options and executive perks, including your very own corner office with a view of the many, many people beneath you.

THE SENATOR RICK SANTORUM

COMPATIBLE BIRTHDAY ★ November_11

You are the proponent of a cause that people want to get behind. Your particular blend of fiscal and environmental policies has gained the backing of many loyal supporters. A run for office and the border are in store for you.

THE CO-ED JV WRESTLING TEAM

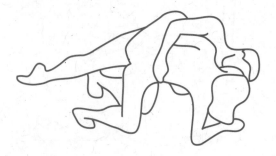

COMPATIBLE BIRTHDAY ★ June_08

Take your opponents down. They have been struggling to be on top for too long. This doesn't mean you have to take them down with force, however. You can also disarm them with joy. Show them such a good time losing that it will be a win-win situation for everyone involved.

THE HIND-QUARTERLY REVIEW

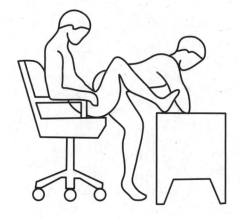

COMPATIBLE BIRTHDAY ★ June_05

They say hindsight is 20/20. And for you it's also a perfect 10.
Looking back at your life, you are able to see the important steps
you took to get ahead and to thoroughly enjoy your great success.

THE CHIROPRACTOR'S SECRET

COMPATIBLE BIRTHDAY ★ August_04

You excel at all that you do. This comes from always being willing to go the distance and bend over backward whenever necessary. You give yourself fully in all that you do, and the people around you appreciate this and reward you accordingly.

WHAT WOULD YOU DO FOR A KLONDIKE BAR?

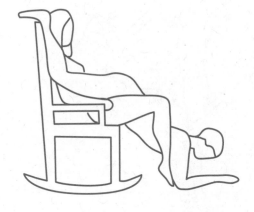

COMPATIBLE BIRTHDAY ★ January_01

You know how to handle the ups and downs of life. You discover that even in solitary confinement, you're not so alone. Here you find yourself and learn that it's more interesting to pay attention to the problems that can't be solved than the ones that can. Keep doing what you're doing and you'll get time out for good behavior before too long.

THE WISH BONE

COMPATIBLE BIRTHDAY ★ October_26

Your personal life may take a nose dive but your finances don't have to. Make sure you diversify your portfolio and keep your chin up. A positive outlook will keep you going strong even in trying situations. Aim high and your investments will deliver rich dividends.

THE WEEKEND AT BERNIE'S

COMPATIBLE BIRTHDAY ★ August_01

Sometimes your job feels like a weekend at Bernie's. But you have the right to remain silent. And sometimes you would be best served to use that right. Plead the fifth, lest you get framed for doing something that can't be undone.

THE EXTENSION CORD

COMPATIBLE BIRTHDAY ★ November_27

You have been called *electric* before and you will be again. Sparks fly when you are near. You are a high-voltage personality and you know how to fire up any situation. Just be careful when plugging in appliances. Power surges like yours have a way of blowing fuses.

ON TOP OF OLD SMOKEY

COMPATIBLE BIRTHDAY ★ April_06

You look incredibly handsome in knee-high stockings. Your legs are the stuff of Rockettes shows and World Cup soccer athletes. When you lift those gorgeous sticks, you'll find you'll rarely need to lift a finger.

THE OUT OF TOWN GUESTS

COMPATIBLE BIRTHDAY ★ October_11

You are a very generous host. You wrap melon balls tenderly in prosciutto. You make little rose decorations out of radishes. And you have a gift for making your guests feel more at home at your house than they do at theirs.

THE RODEO SHOW

COMPATIBLE BIRTHDAY ★ August_31

Face-to-face conversations are where you make your best impressions. Not that you're not adept in groups. But you do excel in one-on-one situations. You make someone feel like they're the only other person in the room (even when you're surrounded by cameras and production assistants).

THE WINDOW WASHER

COMPATIBLE BIRTHDAY ★ June_03

Cleanliness is next to godliness. You will feel like you're in heaven if you take it upon yourself to start to scrub, buff, and polish. While you're at it, do the windows.

DEEPER AND DEEPER

COMPATIBLE BIRTHDAY ★ February_17

Unlike the frightened ostrich, you don't bury your head in the sand.
You take things head on, never shirking from the adventure right in
front of you. Face it, you are a risk-taker spelunking into the magical
dark caves of life's greatest mysteries. So pack your bags and get
ready to see the world. Just don't forget to bring a headlamp.

TONIGHT'S SPECIAL

COMPATIBLE BIRTHDAY ★ September_03

You are a bit of a foodie. You have a taste for exotic dishes. Truffle oil, pheasant, and those delightful little Vienna sausages frequently grace your table. You can also eat a bit too much. But people won't stop loving you just because you're getting fat.

THE "MY WHAT BIG EYES YOU HAVE"

COMPATIBLE BIRTHDAY ★ January _16

Beauty is in the eye of the beholder: One man's beauty is another man's trash. And what you behold is beautiful, even if you are the only one who has the power to see it. Treasure your gift. Like a seagull, you will find joy in a stale old french fry left in an abandoned parking lot.

THE DRAGONFLY

COMPATIBLE BIRTHDAY ★ December_31

A dragonfly is a gorgeous creature. Like the dragonfly, you are not of this world but of someplace else. You have flown in from distant celestial bodies to be here in this plane of existence. People see you as exotic, magical. You could use this image to become a sensational exotic dancer.

LAP OF LUXURY

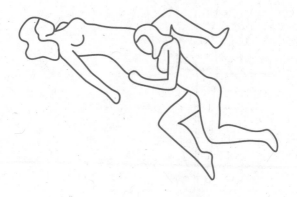

COMPATIBLE BIRTHDAY ★ September_04

You believe that there is plenty in this world to go around. Enough is enough. So you give generously of your time and talents, never worrying about anyone encroaching on your territory. This land is your land. This land is her land. This land was made for you and she.

THE "IT'S A BOY"

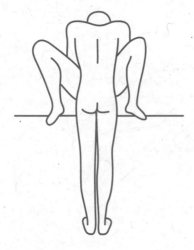

COMPATIBLE BIRTHDAY ★ February_28

You know how to stand and deliver. That's why you are so successful. You handle things with care and know how to bring a large package to the correct recipient in a timely manner (even if you're forced to wear brown polyester).

THE CROWDED SUBWAY

COMPATIBLE BIRTHDAY ★ May_28

Your ability to stand out in a crowd has led you to attract many beautiful people from across a crowded room. But you have no interest in meeting people this way. You'd prefer to meet your true love on Facebook instead.

THE DEPRESSED DOGGIE

COMPATIBLE BIRTHDAY ★ January_08

Even when you're feeling down, you never get too behind in your life. You know how to take the lows with the highs, and that in sadness there is beauty. You call this the beautiful sadness. Yin to yang. Pain to pleasure. The deeper you go into the darkness, the more ecstatic enlightenment you will encounter.

THE THIS LITTLE PIGGY

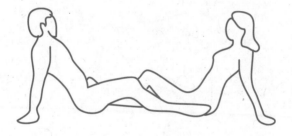

COMPATIBLE BIRTHDAY ★ November_24

You keep a good toehold in life. Even when you lose your footing, you always maintain your composure. You laughed the first time you stubbed your toe and someone suggested you call a toe truck. The second time you heard it, you still laughed, even as you fell to your own brutal demise.

THE "WE'RE NOT WORTHY"

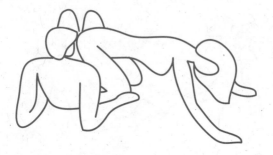

COMPATIBLE BIRTHDAY ★ July_26

You are the most fun person at any party, hands down. People rely on you to pick the music, the color of the napkins, and the kind of icing on the cake. Heck, you are the icing on the cake. You spread your sweetness around for everyone to enjoy. Considering the peaking effect you have on people's blood sugar levels, it's no wonder you're at the top of the list for the next party.

THE INSIDE VIEW

COMPATIBLE BIRTHDAY ★ September_29

If seeing is believing, you are a true believer. You have seen it all and come back to talk about it. A sensitive soul, your eyes are open to the beauty and tragedy all around you. Keep your eyes on the prize and you'll come out a winner in the end.

MARCH_23

WATCHING THE BOOB TUBE

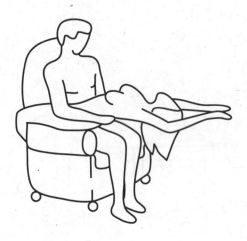

COMPATIBLE BIRTHDAY ★ June_14

Sometimes you just need to get something off your chest. It's important that you do this regularly. You can't carry the weight of the world upon your bosom. Freedom is knocking. Don't just lie there. Aren't you going to get up and answer the door?

THE GOOD SPANKING

COMPATIBLE BIRTHDAY ★ July_05

You've never been one for corporal punishment. But sometimes you just have to slap your hand down to make a point. And you are making an important one. Just because you are a pacifist doesn't mean you can't occasionally "pass a fist" yourself.

THE HEAD OVER HEELS

COMPATIBLE BIRTHDAY ★ December_21

Looking down on people is never a good way to go about things—unless you really are above them and they are beneath you. And sometimes, for better or for worse, this is the case. Just remember to look down graciously, with respect and admiration, and you will never seem arrogant.

YOU'RE HIRED

COMPATIBLE BIRTHDAY ★ October_21

Pay your dues early in your career. Making coffee and photocopies for the right people will get you on the fast track to middle management. Instead of kissing up and kicking down, though, you are good to all those you work with. This is also a boon to your career. "Team-building exercise" is your middle name.

WHEN HARRY MET SALLY AND FRANK

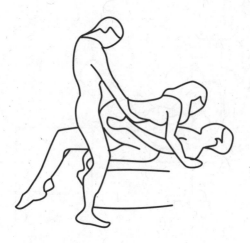

COMPATIBLE BIRTHDAY ★ October_09

The reason the BLT is your favorite sandwich is because of the opportunity for three distinct tastes and textures to come together in one harmonious bite. Crunchy and salty meets crispy and cold meets fat and juicy—filling you up and keeping you interested as you chew. Remember to choose your bread wisely or you'll end up being toast.

THE MARY LOU RETTON

COMPATIBLE BIRTHDAY ★ December_18

To everything there is a season, and a time for every former gymnastic camp experience to pay off under heaven. Use the powder on your hands before you spring into action, and you'll land this one and stick it. A 9.6. Good show.

THE CAN I PLEASE TURN AROUND NOW?

COMPATIBLE BIRTHDAY ★ August_28

Making ends meet has always been something you've been able to do. Now go for something more. Aim high and your wildest dreams can come true. Now is a time where you are not just surviving. Your destiny is for thriving.

THE COMPLEXITY OF DESIRE

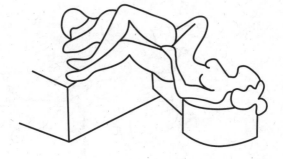

COMPATIBLE BIRTHDAY ★ December_23

Why did you have to go and make things so complicated? Things are often easier than you make them. Keep it simple, silly. Less is more. And once you learn that lesson, you'll quickly follow it up with the lesson that no good deed goes unpunished—especially when that good deed is performed simply and with a whip.

THE HEADACHE CURE

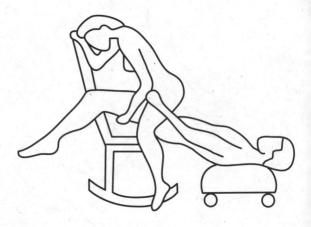

COMPATIBLE BIRTHDAY ★ July_25

Everybody hurts sometimes. But don't worry your pretty little head about it. This too shall pass. And one day, you will live a life beyond song lyrics, things your grandfather used to say, and the occasional quote from you-don't-know-where in the Bible.

THE SNOWBALL EFFECT

COMPATIBLE BIRTHDAY ★ July_17

You are on a roll. Life is gathering momentum and you are moving full speed ahead. Keep in mind that the rolling stone gathers no moss. And by that I mean if you keep spending all of your money on cheap beer and women, you'll never save up enough to buy that moss-colored velvet couch from Crate & Barrel.

TIT FOR TAT

COMPATIBLE BIRTHDAY ★ May_31

You've earned a lot of rewards points lately, and it's time to take a hard-earned vacation for your money well spent. Pack light, as bringing too much will make your suitcase impossible to close. And if you have to buy something like a toothbrush, sweater, or jewel-encrusted octopus on your travels, your credit card will back you up and deliver more delicious rewards.

COME AND KNOCK ON OUR DOOR

COMPATIBLE BIRTHDAY ★ June_11

Come and knock on our door. The world is waiting for you! Where the kisses are hers and hers and his, you'll find you're in good company, too. You may have some issues with landlords along the way. Keep paying your rent on time and make friends with the super and you're golden.

CALLING THE MAYTAG MAN

COMPATIBLE BIRTHDAY ★ August_25

The stains on your reputation will likely fade with time. All things come out in the wash, so make sure you empty your pockets. Stay on top of things, lest you air your dirty laundry, loose change, and poems inscribed on gum wrappers to the world—or to all the people at the laundromat.

THE CYCLING TEAM

COMPATIBLE BIRTHDAY ★ December_30

You have always felt comfortable in a crowd, fully embracing the idea that there is safety in numbers. You like to blend in. Being inconspicuous, people find you nonthreatening, and you find yourself invited into many wonderful and pleasing situations.

APRIL_06

"AHHHCTION!"

COMPATIBLE BIRTHDAY ★ March_08

Always an appreciator of great films, you discover you have a knack for making films yourself. Whether you're acting, directing actors, or recording audio, you manage to create a world-class piece of cinema. You are seriously ready for your close-up and/or money shot. And the reviews will say, "Two thumbs way up!"

THE THRILLER

COMPATIBLE BIRTHDAY ★ August_10

You get your kicks in things most people find morbid. It's this very morbid curiosity that keeps your life interesting. Having embraced the idea of death, you come happily into your own life and the lives of those you touch.

THE CIRQUE DE HO-LAY

COMPATIBLE BIRTHDAY ★ February_24

In the three-ring circus of life, you will find that walking on a tightrope is one of the hardest things one can do. Get off of that wire and try something else. Perhaps the clown car. Or even better, tame a lion or two.

THE TOURIST ATTRACTION

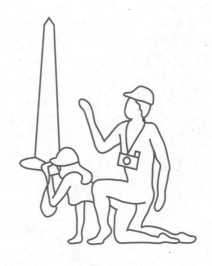

COMPATIBLE BIRTHDAY ★ July_02

Monuments exist to commemorate big people with big dreams who laid out big plans. You take notice of these greats and internalize their greatness. You too can accomplish very big things, and statues will be built and later toppled in your honor.

TAKE THIS AND CALL ME IN THE MORNING

COMPATIBLE BIRTHDAY ★ July_21

You've tried vitamins, exercise, and over-the-counter medications, none of which have cured you. The symptoms you've been having can only be properly treated by a true professional. Someone who specializes in the heart will do your ticker a world of good.

THE GREEN THUMB

COMPATIBLE BIRTHDAY ★ September_14

You've tiptoed through the tulips and danced in fields of daisies. But
nothing makes you quite as happy as sowing seeds in fertile soils.
To the amazement of your neighbors, your garden really flourishes.
When they ask, "How does your garden grow?" you never tell them
of the silver bells and cockle shells and pretty maids all in a row.

ONE HUMP OR TWO?

COMPATIBLE BIRTHDAY ★ November_02

A high tea for two is a delightful way to spend an afternoon with someone you care about. Get to know how many lumps of sugar your companion likes and if they take milk or not. It's these little but important details that will make your teatime quality "we" time.

"STROKE, STROKE, STROKE"

COMPATIBLE BIRTHDAY ★ November_18

Teach a man to fish and he will eat for a lifetime. Give a man a boat and he will row in it for a lifetime (or until he runs out of water). Fortunately for you, you know how to fish and you have a boat. Now just find the right stream to put into and you will live merrily, merrily, merrily, merrily, just like a dream.

THE BEEF BURRITO

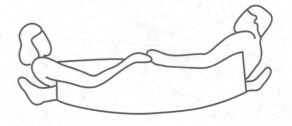

COMPATIBLE BIRTHDAY ★ January_31

You feel contained and cozy in your life, all wrapped up like a pig in a blanket. This undercover operating style makes you well suited to the life of a spy. Just don't let yourself get wound up too tightly or let anyone blow your cover.

THE ACCIDENT WAITING TO HAPPEN

COMPATIBLE BIRTHDAY ★ January_10

Though you prefer acupuncture and homeopathic remedies, modern medicine was created to help us all avoid uncomfortable situations. After all, from Plan B to Band-Aids, sometimes science has got your back.

THE EASY BAKE LOVIN'

COMPATIBLE BIRTHDAY ★ November_17

As a child you found endless delight in peek-a-boo and paddy cake. And then you grew up to become a baker's man, or an assistant to the pastry chef at Chez Panisse. Your skills creating confections have made your life sweet and cream-filled, like a beautiful, fresh cannoli.

THE PYRAMID SCHEME

COMPATIBLE BIRTHDAY ★ November_01

One is the loneliest number. And two is a little less so. But three really is the charm. And you charm the pants off of people with your one wonderful self.

THE HAPPY HAMSTER

COMPATIBLE BIRTHDAY ★ September_08

The work-a-day life can be monotonous. Sometimes you feel like you're running in place. But this isn't always a bad thing. Keep on moving forward and you'll find you will get where you need to go— and if you don't, you'll at least be in better shape for having tried.

THE SLIDE RIGHT IN

COMPATIBLE BIRTHDAY ★ August_11

When you have feelings for a person, it's best not to call them names or chase them around the playground. That may have worked in grade school. Now you have to embrace a whole new strategy. Be a gentleman (or a lady, as the case may be), and you will find yourself sliding right in.

THE SPECIAL DELIVERY

COMPATIBLE BIRTHDAY ★ December_25

Neither rain, nor snow, nor sleet, nor hail can stop you from delivering your package on time. For this reason, you are a top-notch pen pal. And with e-mail, there's no knowing what levels your correspondence will reach.

THE BANANARAMA

COMPATIBLE BIRTHDAY ★ June_23

A healthful diet of fresh fruit will give you all of the potassium, fiber, and antioxidants you need to be happy and healthy. You are what you eat. And your fruit is so fresh, everyone finds you ripe and appealing.

APRIL_22

THE BUBBLE BOY

COMPATIBLE BIRTHDAY ★ December_08

The mark of sophistication is excellence. Excellence is the key to success. And success is what you'd have a chance of having, if only you'd stop playing with supermarket toys at inappropriate times.

CRACKING THE BOOKS

COMPATIBLE BIRTHDAY ★ February_20

Reading makes a person smarter. It stimulates the mind and opens up neurological pathways that allow for new thoughts, ideas, and critical thinking. These things will come to you. But first you must focus on becoming literate. Though you can't yet decipher this, you'll soon learn that reading really is fundamental.

THE B-BOY

COMPATIBLE BIRTHDAY ★ November_19

You haven't heard a good mix tape in awhile. It's about time you make one. Keep your beats old school. And pump up the volume so the whole neighborhood can get a whiff of those breaks. Your electric boogaloo will draw a crowd and a hat full of change.

THE PAINT JOB

COMPATIBLE BIRTHDAY ★ December_02

You are climbing the ladder on the way to great success. Keep
a steady footing and refrain from stepping on any toes on your
journey up, and you will make those above you and those beneath
you quite happy.

APRIL_26

THE PINNED TAIL

COMPATIBLE BIRTHDAY ★ June_09

Your efforts are valiant, but sometimes you have to give up and accept that a donkey doesn't always need a tail. Just like a fish doesn't need a bicycle, even if it tells you that it wants one.

APRIL_27

THE TOTEM HOLE

COMPATIBLE BIRTHDAY ★ August_21

Things are stacking up rather nicely for you of late. Your ducks are all in a row. And to be frank, it doesn't hurt that you also happen to be smart, good-looking, and stacked and/or well-hung.

THE BRIGHT IDEA

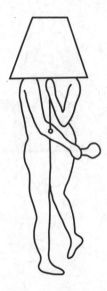

COMPATIBLE BIRTHDAY ★ January_20

Partying with a lampshade on your head is a bit of a cliché, but that doesn't mean it's not fun. Similarly, just because you're not the first person to have an idea doesn't make that idea any less brilliant. Except if that idea entails sticking a light bulb into something other than a light fixture (unless you enjoy visiting the Emergency Room).

THE FRENCH MAID

COMPATIBLE BIRTHDAY ★ October_29

You can't live your life in a vacuum. You must engage with the world.
But do take time out to enjoy your happy corner of this existence.
And while you're there, make sure you keep it clean—but beware the
hose attachment. All of the stories you've heard are true.

THE SLUMBER PARTY

COMPATIBLE BIRTHDAY ★ August_07

It's never right to resort to violence. But a little pillow fight never hurt anyone—except that time your tooth got broken and your dog lost an eye. It was all fun and games until then.

THE EASY RIDER

COMPATIBLE BIRTHDAY ★ July_15

Scooter? You hardly even know her! But that doesn't stop you. Neither does the fact that you've never ridden a bicycle, much less a motorized two-wheeled vehicle.

HOW I LEARNED TO STOP WORRYING

COMPATIBLE BIRTHDAY ★ August_23

You are the bomb. And you know it. Others may not see it that way, however. They may try to keep you down, but you know they're secretly riding your style. Just don't let it give you a 10-gallon head.

THE KENTUCKY DERBY

COMPATIBLE BIRTHDAY ★ June_10

Sometimes being small is a disadvantage. But sometimes it can
be the advantage you need to win the race. To some this might
seem like a gamble. But those that place their bets on you are the
winners. The lesson: You don't need to be hung like a horse to have
a good race.

THE BUTTERNUT SQUASH

COMPATIBLE BIRTHDAY ★ December_13

The soup of the day is a nice cup of you. You know how to serve it up and dish it out. You serve the world with heaping ladles of love. They eat it up and keep coming back for seconds. Be careful what you cook though, lest you give your guests a case of heartburn.

THE RING AROUND HIS ROSY

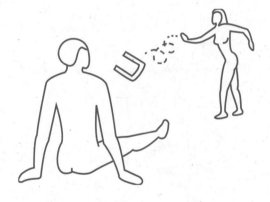

COMPATIBLE BIRTHDAY ★ September_30

You have the luck of the Irish, regardless of your ethnic heritage. You toss off bad mojo in favor of good fortune. Some say you are a dead ringer for Frank Sinatra. Ring a ding ding. And luck be a lady tonight.

THE STRAIGHT SHOOTER

COMPATIBLE BIRTHDAY ★ December_12

You have good aim and always aim to please. And this brings you great rewards as long as you don't shoot the moon.

LIVIN' ON THE EDGE

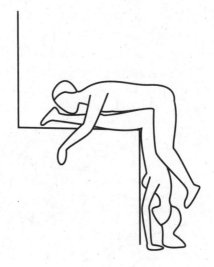

COMPATIBLE BIRTHDAY ★ November_28

Take things as they come and you'll eventually reach that place you dream of . . . too bad it's a third-floor walk-up. There may be some obstacles along the way—but keep persevering and when you finally make it to the top, you'll be sitting pretty.

THE UNDERSTUDY

COMPATIBLE BIRTHDAY ★ April_08

You have crawled your way from obscurity into fame. This is due equally to your tenacity and to the creative, well-lit videos you posted on YouTube. Thanks to your hard work, your acting skills are improving with every take. Keep up the good work and you'll keep rising to the top.

THE BOB VILA

COMPATIBLE BIRTHDAY ★ December_28

You were a curious and talented child—always taking things apart.
And then you put them back together. You have good tools and
excellent craftsmanship. Who needs a professional? You give DIY a
really good name.

THE RAIN OR SHINE

COMPATIBLE BIRTHDAY ★ February_02

The Weather Channel is a great resource. But you can't let your life be ruled by a meteorological television channel. Sometimes you just have to shut it off and go about your business, rain or shine.

STILTED LOVE

COMPATIBLE BIRTHDAY ★ June_30

Love will take you higher than you've ever been lifted before. You rise above the hordes of regular people and see above the crowds. From your vantage point, you are the only two people in the world . . . except for that lady standing nearby. Best to either ignore her or ask her to take a photo with your new digital camera.

THE TOMB RAIDER

COMPATIBLE BIRTHDAY ★ August_30

The ancient Egyptians were buried with their most important earthly possessions, so they could bring them into the afterlife. Thankfully for you, this practice has been discontinued. Had you lived in ancient times, you would have been much beloved by the Egyptians—they would have had you buried alive beside them in the pyramids.

"ALL IN!"

COMPATIBLE BIRTHDAY ★ June_06

You keep your cards close to your chest. And your poker face would fool even the professionals (and you don't have to wear sunglasses to do it). Now, know when to hold 'em and when to fold 'em. And ante up when it's your turn. You've got a winning hand.

THE DA VINCI LOAD

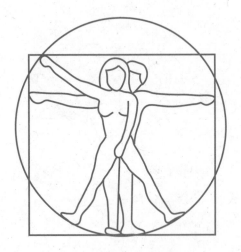

COMPATIBLE BIRTHDAY ★ July_14

Leonardo da Vinci was a man of the Renaissance—a scientist, mathematician, engineer, inventor, anatomist, painter, sculptor, architect, botanist, musician, poet, and writer. He imagined flying machines. Though you have none of these talents, if you borrow some of his inspiration you may not experience universal genius, but you'll have a better chance of seeing the Mona Lisa smile.

THE BUNGEE CORD

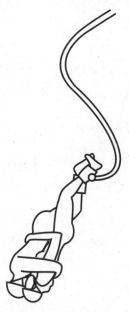

COMPATIBLE BIRTHDAY ★ February_23

You leap before you look. Jumping into things with both feet is a
good way to commit to what you're doing. (It's also a good way
to ruin a perfectly nice pair of shoes.) Invest in a good helmet and
safety harness and you'll enjoy a nice bounce on the cord.

THE GYMNASTICS COACH

COMPATIBLE BIRTHDAY ★ April_16

You are a person of great determination. When you set your mind to something, you make it happen. And the kinds of things you make happen are awe-inspiring and magical.

THE LOVE TRIANGLE

COMPATIBLE BIRTHDAY ★ October_01

Needs, needs, needs—everybody has needs. And you are no
exception to this rule. It's nice of you to try and meet other people's
needs, but sometimes you've got to feed your own.

THE FULL SERVICE SALON

COMPATIBLE BIRTHDAY ★ December_09

You have to love yourself before anyone else is going to love you.
You also have to groom yourself before anyone is going to love you.
Start with your nails. Consider getting waxed. Once you've created
a proper regimen, you'll be very pleased with the results.

CLEANUP IN AISLE FIVE

COMPATIBLE BIRTHDAY ★ October 07

There are some days you feel like going out for dinner, either ordering an entrée or à la carte. Beware of the days you decide to go shopping and try to cook for yourself, however. You're likely to break someone's heart. Or stomach.

SHARE AND SHARE ALIKE

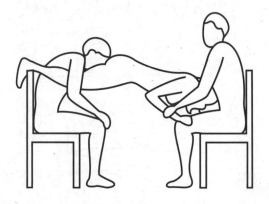

COMPATIBLE BIRTHDAY ★ August_14

One must give to give—not for what one might receive in return.
Thankfully, to give is to receive. And you give a lot of yourself. Your
spirit of generosity gives back to you in spades.

THE STUDY BUDDY

COMPATIBLE BIRTHDAY ★ September_16

It's good to have your head in a book. Reading makes you smarter.
And sharing what you've learned with others reinforces your knowledge.
You may also want to think about teaching. It's a great way to share
all that stuff in your head with those who want to be educated.

THE TREE BUGGER

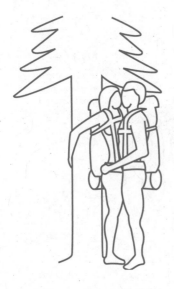

COMPATIBLE BIRTHDAY ★ September_10

A naturalist at heart, you've always known how to enjoy the spoils of Mother Nature. Whether bird watching, hiking, or pitching a tent, you always have a feel-good time outside. Keep an eye out for poisonous plants—try not to lie down in them, and have some calamine lotion close at hand.

THE IRONING BOARD

COMPATIBLE BIRTHDAY ★ June_07

Some perceive you as stiff. But you know this is only half of the story. Deep down, you are a wild, crazy, and fun-loving individual. You just like to get the job done first. And once it's done, you really know how to let loose.

THE HALFTIME SHOW

COMPATIBLE BIRTHDAY ★ January_24

You march to the beat of a different drummer. Having little success as a one-man band, you find you prefer to play in an ensemble. This still allows you to play a mean solo every now and again. And you've learned that both melody and harmony make for a full-bodied song.

THE CHAIN BANG

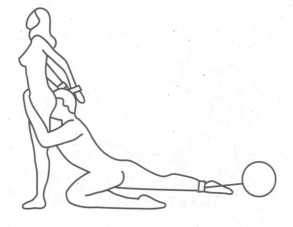

COMPATIBLE BIRTHDAY ★ July_28

You've broken some laws and some hearts and now you're doing time. Your correctional officer keeps you under house arrest. Nothing says strength like a person who perseveres and doesn't allow this to hold them back. You will get off for good behavior sooner than you might think.

GUTTER BALLING

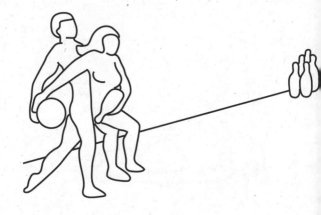

COMPATIBLE BIRTHDAY ★ December_15

You know how to keep score. But does this get in the way of you rolling with things? Spare yourself the tally of who did what to whom. This will pin you down. If you have a good set of balls, you can strike it big. Just consider getting some disinfectant spray for your shoes.

STOP IN THE NAME OF LOVE

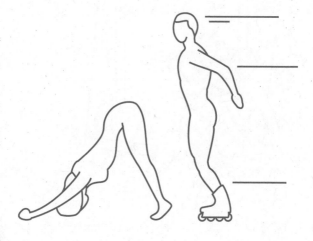

COMPATIBLE BIRTHDAY ★ September_25

Have you ever seen those guys rollerblading in Central Park? The ones in the fruit boots? You know the ones. When it comes to them, my friend, you have a gift. Like turning water into wine, you can turn gay to straight and straight to gay. Use your powers for good and you will skate through life quite happily.

THE WINDOW TREATMENT

COMPATIBLE BIRTHDAY ★ March_18

Some people don't do windows. You've always found this approach to life to be misguided and a little pathetic. Why would you want to limit yourself? If you get a chance to do a window, you do it. You really do. And you only leave a few streaks, and take a few peeks.

THE HUNGRY HUNGRY HIPPO

COMPATIBLE BIRTHDAY ★ January_14

Good things happen to good people. And you are good. Not surprisingly, good, strong people are drawn to you, and will lift you up into even higher planes of creativity and imagination.

THE 19TH HOLE

COMPATIBLE BIRTHDAY ★ January_03

Golf metaphors and jokes generally only mean something to balding, middle-aged businessmen. Thankfully for you, this is who you are—at least at heart. So which club are you going to use? Might we suggest the driver?

THE EYE CONTACT

COMPATIBLE BIRTHDAY ★ April_02

When you make a toast, make sure you look your compatriot in the eye. If you don't, the result could be seven years of regrettable intercourse. And if you do look them in the eye, you may just get lucky right there on the spot.

JUNE_01

VERY CASUAL FRIDAYS

COMPATIBLE BIRTHDAY ★ May_13

If you do what you love, the money will soon follow. So keep on doing what you're doing. Success is yours to be had. Enjoy the fruits of your labor.

STICKING IT TO THE MAN

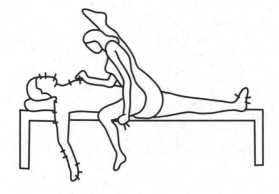

COMPATIBLE BIRTHDAY ★ January_04

You know what it's like to be on pins and needles. And it's really not as bad as most people think. You've found peace and healing reading the Tao Te Ching. Lao Tzu is your man and Eastern medicine, your healer. Now if only you could figure out the sound of one hand clapping. (Hint: Sounds like a bunch of wind.)

THE MAC DADDY

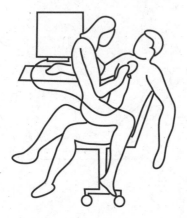

COMPATIBLE BIRTHDAY ★ March_13

The IT department at your company may have been outsourced to India, but that hasn't gotten in the way of getting your machine serviced. You've hired your own one-person geek squad to troubleshoot all of your hard-drive needs.

"COME HERE OFTEN?"

COMPATIBLE BIRTHDAY ★ October_25

Take a good look around you, and you'll notice that there are other people in this world—living, breathing, working, and taking pleasure from all the same things as you. This is a beautiful and many-splendored thing. Though we may not feel quite as unique as we once thought we were, at least we know we're not quite so alone.

THANK GOD FOR GLASS COFFEE TABLES

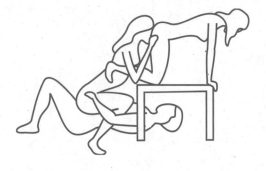

COMPATIBLE BIRTHDAY ★ March_02

A house is not a home until it has a coffee table in it you really like and can live with. You will be most contented with one made out of glass. Just don't fall on the sharp corners. And when you put liquids on your new table remember to use a nice set of coasters.

OH, THE PLACES YOU'LL GO

COMPATIBLE BIRTHDAY ★ February_06

Congratulations! You have just graduated to a new level of self-actualization. Oh, the places you'll go! Such fabulous, magnificent, dark, and moist places!

THE CAPITAL L

COMPATIBLE BIRTHDAY ★ May_23

You come at things from a different angle than most people. This gives you a unique vantage point. This singular way of yours makes you outstanding in your field.

THE FOOT-LONG

COMPATIBLE BIRTHDAY ★ February_25

You're an all-beef kind of person, no bones about it. Just be conscientious when putting your beef on a bun. A high-protein diet is quickly ruined by too many carbs. Carbs aren't all bad, though. So enjoy them when you have them. Relish your delicious opportunities.

JUNE_09

THE SNAKE CHARMER

COMPATIBLE BIRTHDAY ★ April_26

You've always been good at dealing with difficult people. Some
have even called you a snake charmer. You win over even the
most venomous of opponents, who try to scare the pants off you.
Be careful. Those trouser snakes may try to get you when your
defenses are down.

THE SWING AND A KISS

COMPATIBLE BIRTHDAY ★ April_14

You have no need for a pinch hitter in life. You pitch your balls and you hit them too. You make it to first base. And skip right to third base before sliding in for a home run. Keep your eye on the ball and you'll have nothing to worry about. You're in a league all your own.

THE X FACTOR

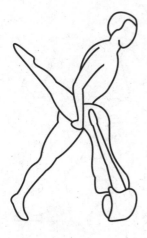

COMPATIBLE BIRTHDAY ★ December_07

X marks the spot. And you are there at the cross-hatch. It's an exciting place to be—even if the MPAA gave you an X-rating.

THE NIP AND DIP

COMPATIBLE BIRTHDAY ★ December_04

Modern art has always confused you. You find yourself in museums and galleries shaking your head and saying, "I just don't get it." What you need to do is embrace the art form itself. Don't try to make sense of it. Just experience it. Feel it. Create it. Be it. Before you know it, you'll be an art appreciator of the deepest kind.

JUNE_13

THE MARATHON MAN

COMPATIBLE BIRTHDAY ★ January_12

Try as you might, sometimes you can't run away from your problems. What are you running from, anyway? No matter how fast you go it's still right there in front of you. It's time you dealt with your dilemma head on. Stop and be still and you'll find you had the answers right there all the time, too.

THE PARTY OF ONE

COMPATIBLE BIRTHDAY ★ March_23

You've partied with the best of them. But when it comes right down to it, you are the best of them. Who needs to leave the house when you already have all you need? Put on your party hat and don some fun—you've personally been invited to a party of one. (Don't forget to RSVP.)

THE JACK AND JILL

COMPATIBLE BIRTHDAY ★ November_14

Life is full of peaks and valleys. Learn to take the highs with the lows. Just keep on climbing both the mountains and molehills before you and you will reach your peak at just the right time.

THE CRANK YANKER

COMPATIBLE BIRTHDAY ★ February_15

Today is not a good day to prank call your family. Leave those poor people alone. Pull someone else's leg for a change. You'll find without your family in the mix, you'll have a whole other kind of good time.

THE MOMMY DEAREST

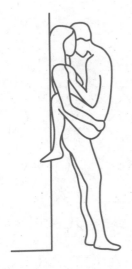

COMPATIBLE BIRTHDAY ★ Apri_03

We all need to be held sometimes. It's okay to need that. It's when you start clinging desperately like a wounded monkey that things really get kind of weird. Loosen your grip on life and learn to let go.

MAKING THE LIST

COMPATIBLE BIRTHDAY ★ November_23

Getting into great parties and the best restaurants takes skill, panache, and good connections. You have all of these things, and will always be at the head of the line. Make sure you choose a fun "plus one" you can see yourself spending the rest of the night with.

THE SLOTHS

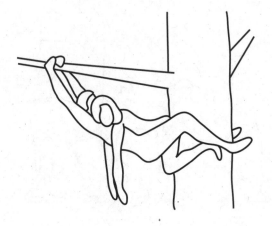

COMPATIBLE BIRTHDAY ★ January_29

Through great efforts and flexibility, you are really coming into your own this year. Whether you're in a twist, a bind, or a pickle, you manage to come out on top. Stay loose and anything is possible.

THE CRAFTY PODIATRIST

COMPATIBLE BIRTHDAY ★ January_17

Birds know how to fly and bees know how to buzz. But what do you know how to do? Well, you're inventive. You come up with new things and do them. You take things into your own hands and have a very satisfying time doing it. It's enough to give you a buzz and make you feel like you're flying.

CHECKMATE

COMPATIBLE BIRTHDAY ★ August_18

You can learn to play chess in a day, but the game takes a lifetime to master. For example, if you take your opponent's queen, that doesn't necessarily mean you'll win. Just remember to keep your head in the game and play through to the end.

THE LEG PRESS

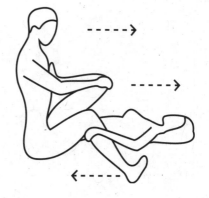

COMPATIBLE BIRTHDAY ★ March_31

Exercise your right to exercise. Maybe you've gotten a little thick in the thighs or a little wide in the waist. This is a thing only you can solve. And it doesn't have to be a drag. Being fit can be fun!

JUNE_23

THE RIM JOB

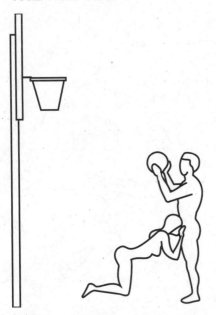

COMPATIBLE BIRTHDAY ★ April_21

You got game. You always bang the boards when you take your shot, after driving through a full-court press with penetration. The way you play, you're a slam-dunk to win.

SYNCHRONIZED RIMMING

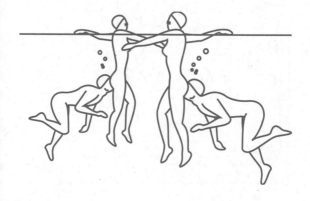

COMPATIBLE BIRTHDAY ★ .February_10

The swim team was never really your thing. You never liked the
crawl or the breast stroke, though the side stroke was kind of nice.
But your fear of the deep end made you better suited to more
shallow pursuits, like synchronized swimming. With things a little
less deep, whether you sink or swim is completely up to you.

THE BOX LUNCH

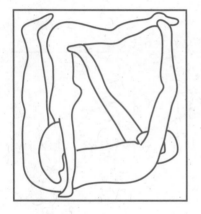

COMPATIBLE BIRTHDAY ★ July_16

The expression "think outside the box" seems really overused and pretty lame to you. Why think outside of something that you can think inside of so clearly? Its parameters are defined. If the box is big enough, you know where you stand and where to be in there. Hey, whatever works for you, man. Whatever.

A WALK TO REMEMBER

COMPATIBLE BIRTHDAY ★ February_21

You enjoy doing things in a memorable way. You take walks to remember. You eat breakfasts to remember. Sometimes you put a little hat on your pancakes. Then you take a picture of that cute, bonnet-wearing stack and put it in your scrapbook. You have a special way of bringing this kind of meaning to flapjacks. Always a creator of a fond memory.

THE HALL MONITOR

COMPATIBLE BIRTHDAY ★ September_23

Are you feeling a little stuck lately? Like you don't know where you are or how you got there? It's OK. You'll soon get out of this jam—right?

HIKING THE BALLS

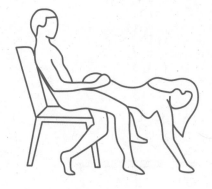

COMPATIBLE BIRTHDAY ★ July_07

Being a cheerleader or on the football team in high school was really good for your popularity. Everybody knew you and wanted to be like you. Now that high school is over, you still expect the same attention. Thankfully for you, middle-aged housewives and balding fat men get noticed, too.

THE IN-FLIGHT SNACK

COMPATIBLE BIRTHDAY ★ December_19

The sky is falling. Oh no—wait a minute. That's you. You're rising.
The sky is right where it's always been. Keep aiming for the moon, and
you're sure to land on your neighbor's roof.

THE RISING TIDE

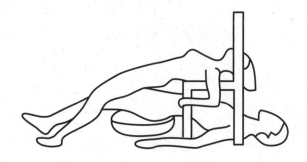

COMPATIBLE BIRTHDAY ★ July_24

Some days you feel like you can't get out from under all the things on top of you. If you can embrace this as a part of life, you will find satisfaction all around. Your innovation will get you out from under and back on top again.

RI-CO-LAAAA!

COMPATIBLE BIRTHDAY ★ September_18

As a child, you loved the chocolatey goodness of Swiss Miss. As you grew older, you upgraded to the delightful pleasures of St. Pauli Girl. And now that you're getting that chronic cough, another nice alpine delight will care for you and your lederhosen. *Ri-co-laaaa!*

THE BACK SCRATCHER

COMPATIBLE BIRTHDAY ★ January_09

You have a way of using people to get your needs met. This may sound bad, but it's rather inventive of you, and often gives the other person involved a new and wonderful experience. Just try not to injure anyone in the process.

NUMBER FIVE IS ALIVE!

COMPATIBLE BIRTHDAY ★ August_29

Somewhat of an introvert, your relations with people have always been strained. Yet thanks to technology and the continuous development of the Internet, you've found new outlets in which to stick your joy.

HOW THE LIBERTY BELL GOT ITS CRACK

COMPATIBLE BIRTHDAY ★ August_20

You have always thrust yourself right into the center of the pursuit of liberty, freedom, and happiness. Good for you. That's your right as a citizen. Let some serious freedom ring!

THE HUNGMAN'S DILEMMA

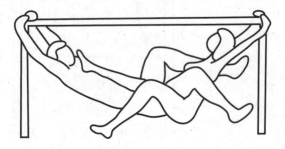

COMPATIBLE BIRTHDAY ★ December_24

People today lead such busy lives. So is it such a bad idea to take a break from all the hustle and bustle and just hang out? No, it's not a bad idea at all. You deserve it. When you relax, the whole world relaxes with you.

THE YOUTUBE

COMPATIBLE BIRTHDAY ★ September_11

Video technology is developing at an incredible rate. And you would be well-advised to jump on that bandwagon. If you've been feeling like a Lonely Girl or a Ninja willing to answer questions, your Internet fame will take care of that. Brace yourself. You're about to get a lot of traffic.

THE ROYAL SCEPTER

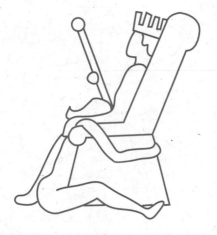

COMPATIBLE BIRTHDAY ★ June_21

You were born into royalty. (Maybe not the British kind—more like the discount warehouse kingdom type.) But you still rule. Be kind to your subjects. And share the crowning abundance of all you have from your throne.

THE ANCHOR MAN

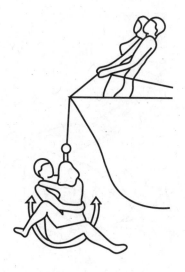

COMPATIBLE BIRTHDAY ★ March_10

Sometimes you go a little overboard in your enthusiasm for things. Cast away this mania and embrace something more solid and better suited to you. This, you'll find, will be a real life preserver.

BEND IT LIKE BECKHAM

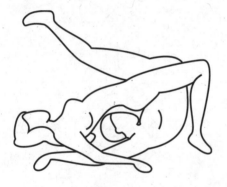

COMPATIBLE BIRTHDAY ★ September_15

You've got a mean kick. And you know how to use it in the right situations. So get out there and start enjoying yourself. It's time to kick up your heels.

THE EVEL KNIEVEL

COMPATIBLE BIRTHDAY ★ October_24

"Stunts" is your middle name. Inspired by the late master of extremes, Evel Knievel, you push things to the limit. You jump over buses and stare death in the face. Plan out your stunts carefully and you'll get where you want to go, and ride happily off into the sunset.

PARTY OF FIVE

COMPATIBLE BIRTHDAY ★ April_25

Not knowing what you're getting into is sometimes the best way to get into something. Being naïve is a virtue. That way you're not blinded by all of the choices in front of you. Just keep groping your way through the dark, and you'll soon get what you seek.

THE POGO CHICK

COMPATIBLE BIRTHDAY ★ December_05

You've been a little lax lately. Sleeping in that extra fifteen minutes. Checking your personal e-mail a few too many times at work. Wearing dirty socks and your underwear inside out. This isn't like you. Deep down, you're a Type A screaming to get out. Unleash your OCD side. Hop to it!

THE CUTE GIRL AT THE GYM

COMPATIBLE BIRTHDAY ★ February_01

Some people go to the gym to work out their biceps. Some people are focused on their pectorals. You like to work out other muscles.

THE SUNBATHER

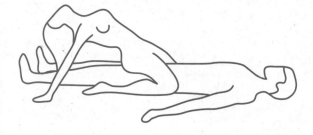

COMPATIBLE BIRTHDAY ★ September_12

Though you lacked significant accomplishments in your youth, you have blossomed as you have gotten older, baring your assets for all the world to see and enjoy until you reach a ripe old age.

JULY_15

CHOOSE YOUR OWN ADVENTURE

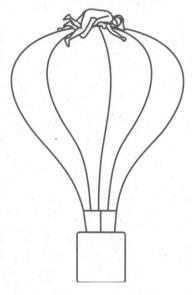

COMPATIBLE BIRTHDAY ★ October_18

You have set off on your own adventure. You've paid the money for it and signed all the releases. You've done this at your own risk and of your own free will. At least you put your money where your mouth is. Some people only talk about doing the things you actually do. So though you may end up dead, at least you're not full of hot air.

EZ-PASS

COMPATIBLE BIRTHDAY ★ June_25

You've been a bit short on cash. Sometimes you have to do what
you have to do in order to get by. Use your talents to your advantage
when you're in a bind. But try not to always resort to your greatest
strengths. This will eventually take its toll.

THE TEAM EFFORT

COMPATIBLE BIRTHDAY ★ May_07

It's usually when you're not out looking for love that it strikes. You're now like a hot plate of fried chicken—everyone wants a piece of you. The good thing is that you can choose who gets the white meat, the dark meat, the drumsticks, and that nice moist breast.

THE INTERNSHIP

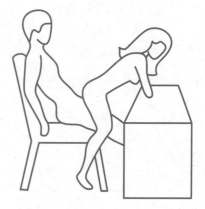

COMPATIBLE BIRTHDAY ★ March_01

You hate your job. Your boss is incompetent. But the job pays your bills and your boss signs the checks. Do what needs to be done to get the job done. And consider going back to school. You'll need a better education to support yourself when you get fired.

THE OLYMPIC MOMENT

COMPATIBLE BIRTHDAY ★ May_18

Someone has something important they'd like to relay to you. Don't run from this. It's something that will help you further along in the race. It's important to keep moving forward, and be able to track all of your important changes.

THE BUZZ ALDRIN

COMPATIBLE BIRTHDAY ★ April_09

One small step for a human can be an incredibly enjoyable step
in the right direction for humanity. Stake your claim on what you
desire. Plant your nation's flag in the rich soil, and call it your own.

THE WASH AND WAX

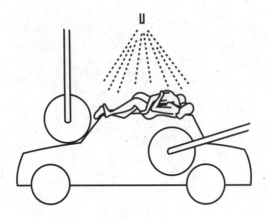

COMPATIBLE BIRTHDAY ★ April_10

You like a clean car and you'll go to any length to get one. You also like it waxed and buffed. When your car is free from dirt and shining, you are quite certain it runs better. You are crazy to think this.

THE RUG BURN

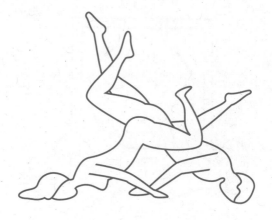

COMPATIBLE BIRTHDAY ★ October_12

Sometimes keeping your head down is the best thing you can do. It can also lead to some serious rug burn on your face. Lift your head up high. And don't worry. Those scabs will heal before you know it.

THE GONG HO

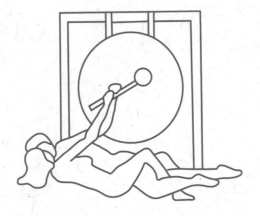

COMPATIBLE BIRTHDAY ★ April_04

Did you ever watch *The Gong Show* when you were a kid? Man, that was a quality show. Too bad it's not on anymore. As an entertainer, you could really stand to take some of that show's cues.

THE CHERRY PICKER

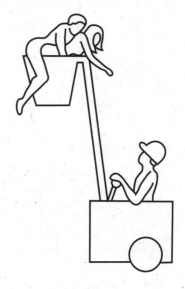

COMPATIBLE BIRTHDAY ★ February_14

You make friends in high places and are providing a valuable service to people, but sometimes you do it at your own risk. But putting yourself in danger to help others has brought you great rewards.

THE LONDON BRIDGES

COMPATIBLE BIRTHDAY ★ January_11

How do you bridge the gap between where you currently are and where you want to be? Get a blueprint and start building those bridges one brick at a time. If you place your building blocks carefully, with your skills, you'll never have to deal with your bridges falling down.

THE SHOCK AND AWE

COMPATIBLE BIRTHDAY ★ March_21

You have your own special way of doing things. Others might not understand what you're up to. They may even criticize you. Just remind them that there's more than one way to skin a cat, even though you know that skinning cats is wrong.

JULY_27

THE HELPING HAND

COMPATIBLE BIRTHDAY ★ January_06

You can get by on your own, but sometimes you need a helping hand. Give yourself a handout every now and again. If you don't drop a quarter in your own cup first, no one else will.

THE Wii

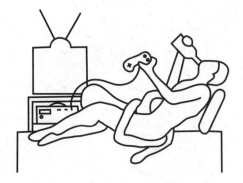

COMPATIBLE BIRTHDAY ★ May_25

You are skilled at a variety of video games. You've put a lot of
time into mastering what you do. So much time that you actually
are a Guitar Hero and you started a real political revolution with
DanceDanceRevolution. Looks like all that time at home in front
of the TV really did pay off.

THE BIG KAHUNA

COMPATIBLE BIRTHDAY ★ November_15

You've always been into surfers. You think the metaphors inherent in surfing make for a really well-grounded, Zen kind of partner. You also like the way the sun bleaches their hair and the way the salt tastes on their skin. Get yourself that Gidget/Gerardo and together you can hang 20.

CATCH ME IF YOU CAN

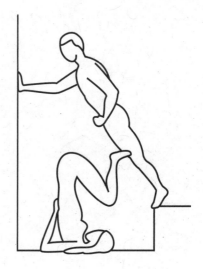

COMPATIBLE BIRTHDAY ★ December_26

That Pilates class you've been taking has been really good for your body and mind. And for your social life. You've even hooked up with people just walking around on the street. Way to be involved, make new friends, and tighten your abs!

THE FINGER ROLL

COMPATIBLE BIRTHDAY ★ May_18

Some people skate through life. And lucky for you, you're one of those people. When it's time for couples' skate, you will pick an able partner, even if he isn't as well-equipped as you are.

BI-CURIOUS GEORGE

COMPATIBLE BIRTHDAY ★ March_06

Whether they're willing to admit it or not, everyone is bisexual. Sexuality exists on a spectrum. Some people just like to suck on genitals that look like their own. You like to mix it up and sample from a buffet of options. You are the quintessential Bi-curious George/Jane.

THE STRAP BANGER

COMPATIBLE BIRTHDAY ★ March_24

You would do well to give up the Escalade. Though it may take a little longer waiting for the subway, think of all the benefits. Lower commuting costs, reduced carbon emissions, and a group of kind strangers—friends you haven't met yet—there to share your mornings with you.

PIG AND A POKE

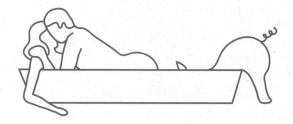

COMPATIBLE BIRTHDAY ★ May_12

Your home is a mess. Your office is a sty. It's like you're part pig or something. This is a turn-off for many. But you'll find those who are turned on by eating out of a trough. Keep your eye out for this kind of lover. Soweeeeee!

AUGUST_04

THE BACKPACKER

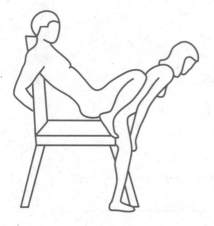

COMPATIBLE BIRTHDAY ★ August_02

Having recently gotten back from hiking in the backwoods, you've found that even the heaviest baggage is quite light. What might be cumbersome to some is merely a "sack of silk stockings" to you. Guess who's gonna be wearing pantyhose later? That's right—you!

THE HAPPY LANDING

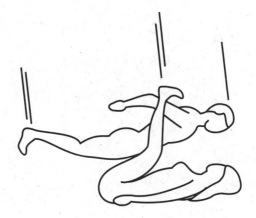

COMPATIBLE BIRTHDAY ★ December_16

You've landed or will soon land yourself a pretty great gig. This will make you happy for a time. And then you'll get restless and start wanting the next big thing, forgetting altogether how great what you've got going now is. Try to appreciate where you are and let the restlessness carry you even further forward.

THE GROUP MOVE

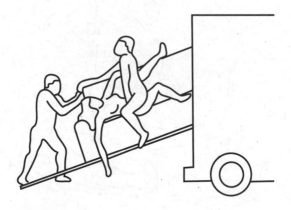

COMPATIBLE BIRTHDAY ★ January_13

Many hands make light work. The more people you have involved in your life to help you do the heavy lifting, the better. And your friends are there for you. You'll be touched to see how eager they are to give you a helping hand. Their generosity will move you.

THE CAN'T STOP, WON'T STOP

COMPATIBLE BIRTHDAY ★ April_30

Last night a DJ saved your life. Dance clubs are the new church, and DJs are the new preachers. Music is our gateway to heaven. It makes the people come together.

THE CHEEK TO CHEEK

COMPATIBLE BIRTHDAY ★ March_28

It's always nice to know that someone's behind you 100 percent, backing you up when you need support. Now's the time to employ those wonderful physical attributes you haven't had a clue what to do with until now.

BULL'S-EYE

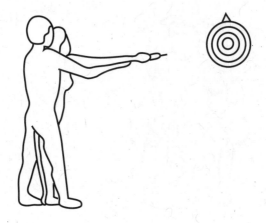

COMPATIBLE BIRTHDAY ★ September_20

Some people throw daggers with their eyes. Not you. You throw darts of kindness at their cold hearts. And you've got good aim. This is a great talent, and makes you popular in bars and among enemies.

THE OPTICAL ILLUSION

COMPATIBLE BIRTHDAY ★ August_05

Things are not always as they seem. And that's good to know—because the way things seem at first glance sometimes isn't half as interesting as what lies below the surface. Keep this in mind when you find out that who you brought home isn't who you thought they were at all. There are optical and other illusions at play. But don't worry. Beauty comes in all kinds of packages. .

THE KOURNIKOVA

COMPATIBLE BIRTHDAY ★ May_08

A little game of back and forth has always made you happy. You are skilled at getting it over the net. But sometimes you're happy to play a singles game. You've got a nice backhand that impresses your opponents. Yet if you placed a wager on the game, people might think it was a racket.

THE FLING AND A PRAYER

COMPATIBLE BIRTHDAY ★ June_12

Some people don't believe in it, but you know the power of prayer. Asking for divine intervention is something you've benefited from. Given all of the things you get away with, you know that someone's smiling down on you.

CO-ED NAKED TUG-OF-WAR

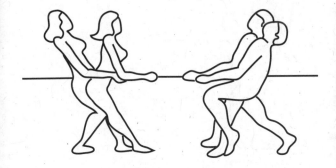

COMPATIBLE BIRTHDAY ★ November_22

If life were a game of tug-of-war you would find yourself on a very capable team with an able-bodied partner. Since life is not a game of tug-of-war, you instead find yourself alone wishing you were at summer camp giving the old one-two-three-pull rope burn.

THE PRIVATES INVESTIGATOR

COMPATIBLE BIRTHDAY ★ June_17

We don't always know what's ahead of us. But we do know what's behind us. And that should give you some comfort. If you don't have a clear sense of things to come, take a little time to evaluate where you've been. You've got to look where it's gone before you can see it coming.

DUMPSTER DIVING

COMPATIBLE BIRTHDAY ★ November_08

"Waste not, want not" is your motto. You find beauty in things others regard as rubbish. For example, as a kid you found that wonderful pet rat in your neighbor's garbage. And you learned the valuable lesson that one person's trash really is another person's treasure.

THE FULL BODY MASSAGE

COMPATIBLE BIRTHDAY ★ October_04

You are a sensualist. You've always believed that a perfect partner would be a chef or a masseuse. Lucky you—you've found someone who is both. Now just keep them from using the olive oil from their kitchen for your massage. Lotion is a magic potion. Especially on crocodile skin like yours.

THE NAUGHTY PROFESSOR

COMPATIBLE BIRTHDAY ★ December_01

You've always enjoyed higher learning. You have or will someday have two master's degrees. People think of you as a smart person. Eighty-seven percent of this impression is due to your glasses.

AUGUST_18

THE TRAPEZE ARTIST

COMPATIBLE BIRTHDAY ★ August_26

The three rings at the circus were created to enable multiple shows to happen simultaneously. But isn't it exciting when these separate shows come together in one dynamic performance? Try combining your talents and see how much fun you'll have with an elephant, a tiger, and sixty-three clowns. Now that's a good show!

MR. CLEAN

COMPATIBLE BIRTHDAY ★ October_28

To put it mildly, you have OCD. You take cleaning to new levels. And you always grab an opportunity to tidy up. You leave no corner unmopped, no lampshade undusted. Though it's a bit tedious and disconcerting to others, you do clean up real good.

THE HURDLER

COMPATIBLE BIRTHDAY ★ August_15

You have made great strides and are hurdling over many challenges. If you're not getting to where you want from where you are, keep on running and jumping and eventually you'll reach that much-desired finish line.

THE STREAKY MIRROR

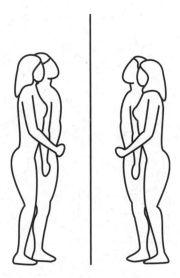

COMPATIBLE BIRTHDAY ★ April_27

The great thing about mirrors is that they reflect us back to ourselves. We can catch a glimpse of what the world sees and make sure our hair isn't too out of place. This self-reflection only becomes a problem when indulged in too much. Watch out for that, Narcissus.

THE SWAN SONG

COMPATIBLE BIRTHDAY ★ August_27

You are all bendy like a straw. You twist this way and that. And just like those straws, you amaze the people who use you.

TABLE FOR TWO

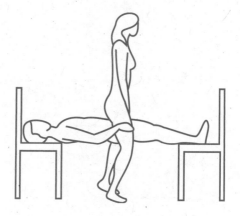

COMPATIBLE BIRTHDAY ★ May_02

Balance in life is one of the most important things a person can strive for. We are all pulled in so many different directions. Be careful not to spread yourself too thin. Give yourself some support and you are certain to live in great harmony with others.

AUGUST_24

THE CLAM DIGGER

COMPATIBLE BIRTHDAY ★ July_10

Some days you don't know where you start and others begin. It's hard to define your boundaries. And that can be a beautiful thing. Except when you're trying to put on a pair of pants. We need boundaries—our own and others—so we can cover our own asses.

THE STARBUCKS

COMPATIBLE BIRTHDAY ★ September_05

The best part of waking up is a delicious hot cup of coffee at home. Nobody does it better than you do. Now the question is, do you prefer one hump or two?

THE PRESSED SANDWICH

COMPATIBLE BIRTHDAY ★ May_22

You'd be hard pressed not to have a good time in most situations.
You're such a relaxed and carefree kind of person that even when you're
in an awkward position you have a way of making things light and fun.

MOVIE NIGHT

COMPATIBLE BIRTHDAY ★ September_07

You're pretty laid-back. And you'd do best to find a partner who is equally as laid-back as you are. It's no good trying to make things work with someone who isn't on your level. It's like forcing a size 8 foot into a size 6 shoe, and knowing you, you'd like to be a little more comfortable than that.

THE AQUARIYUM

COMPATIBLE BIRTHDAY ★ March_29

You are very thankful for the good things in your life. Sometimes you get a little tanked to celebrate it all. Just don't get too carried away with your gratitude. It might seem a little fishy.

THE RUBBER DUCKY

COMPATIBLE BIRTHDAY ★ December_06

It's important to wash thoroughly before going on a date. You never know how well things will go, and you don't want to end up having your date do the dirty work for you.

THE CAMEL HUMP

COMPATIBLE BIRTHDAY ★ May_29

Being a camel jockey is a tough profession. Why would you want to be part of a culture that encourages being exploited by gamblers? Thankfully for you, this isn't your livelihood. You are just enjoying the simple fantasy ride of your life.

THE FIRE HAZARD

COMPATIBLE BIRTHDAY ★ February_09

There's no escaping your true self. You've been trying to be something you're not. As Mark Twain once said, "Be yourself. Everyone else is taken."

THE FRUIT SALAD

COMPATIBLE BIRTHDAY ★ December_22

Eating five fruits and vegetables a day is the key to a healthful diet, according to the U.S. Department of Agriculture's new dietary guidelines. Consume these things in abundance and your load will be much lighter.

DRUM ROLL PLEASE

COMPATIBLE BIRTHDAY ★ January_18

You've always dreamt of playing in a band, and have even gone so far as to post one of those "Bandmates Wanted" ads in your local free paper. You got a few responses, but nothing ever came of it. I guess it would make sense to learn to play an instrument first. Have you considered playing the drums?

SEPTEMBER_03

THE PUPPET MASTER

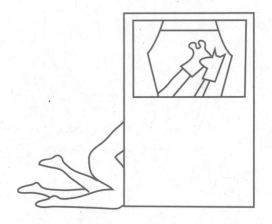

COMPATIBLE BIRTHDAY ★ November_16

Sometimes it's hard to say the things you want to say. Role-playing and using inanimate objects like stuffed animals and hand puppets is sometimes the best way to get it out. In order to communicate the things we need to say on the inside, sometimes we've got to use the tools on the outside.

THE CHICK MAGNET

COMPATIBLE BIRTHDAY ★ March_16

If you're finding that people aren't as attracted to you as you'd like them to be, it's time to take things into your own hands. There are tools you can use and techniques you can try to make yourself more magnetic. Try reading some magazines for tips, and think about a haircut. A little sprucing up never hurt.

SEPTEMBER_05

THE ALL-NIGHT CRAM SESSION

COMPATIBLE BIRTHDAY ★ November_21

Studious to the core, you've made the dean's list several times. It didn't hurt that you have a very special relationship with your dean. But that's not the only thing that's gotten you good marks. You've put in a lot of hard time on your subject. Three words: magna cum loud.

THE CABOOSE GOOSE

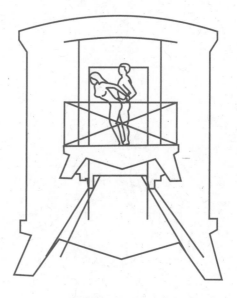

COMPATIBLE BIRTHDAY ★ October_23

You used to be one of those cool kids who rode in the back of the bus. You don't take the bus anymore, but you're still pretty cool. You ride in the back of taxis now. And you've really developed a fondness for the back of a train. You really know how to let loose in a caboose.

THE PILATES HOTTIES

COMPATIBLE BIRTHDAY ★ January_05

What's more important than having a ball? It's sharing your good time with others. And you share and share and share.

THE TIGHT GROPE

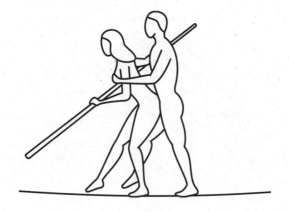

COMPATIBLE BIRTHDAY ★ July_01

Life is often a lot like walking a tight rope. You have to find just the right balance and just the right partner to walk the tenuous path of life with. That and slow, steady steps will get you successfully to the other side.

SEPTEMBER_09

THE A-TEAM

COMPATIBLE BIRTHDAY ★ October_16

You work well in teams—like a SWAT team. Or that team with Mr. T. What was that show called? *The A-Team*! You're an A-Team kind of person. Or maybe you just look a lot like Mr. T.

THE GUILTY PLEASURE

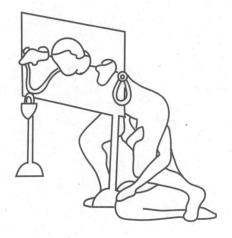

COMPATIBLE BIRTHDAY ★ November_25

You've been guilty of a few crimes and misdemeanors. And you're making up for it and paying your debt to society. You may feel shackled, but you're not dead. Don't let it keep you from taking care of yourself by having a tossed salad or just a good time every once in a while.

THE CRAWL SPACE

COMPATIBLE BIRTHDAY ★ July_06

Living in the city, space is tight. You can't even open your dresser drawers because your bed is too close. Consider a move to the suburbs. Someone's got to start the suburban regentrification process sooner or later.

THE BARBERSHOP DUET

COMPATIBLE BIRTHDAY ★ December_17

You take pride in looking good. And you surround yourself with people who are attractive and make an effort to be that way. But there's more to you than sheer beauty. You are beautiful on the inside, too. All around, you make the cut.

THE HEART TO HEART

COMPATIBLE BIRTHDAY ★ October_02

You're not someone who likes to talk about things. You'd rather just have things be. But sometimes what your relationships need is a good heart to heart. Having an open dialogue with an equally open heart can help you be the best you can be. Or at least lead to some hot, rocking sex.

THE GOLDEN ARCHES

COMPATIBLE BIRTHDAY ★ March_22

As a kid, you loved to eat McDonald's Happy Meals. The toy inside, the delicious little paper bag of fries, the tiny little Coke. You learned early on to love the golden arches. Why? Because McDonald's is delicious. And regardless of any damned movie made by Morgan Spurlock, you keep going back for more.

THE TRIPLE LINDY

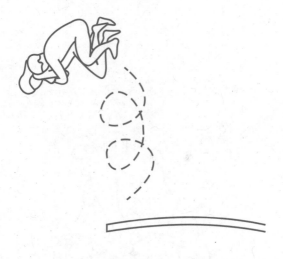

COMPATIBLE BIRTHDAY ★ October_20

Use where you are in your life right now as a springboard to get you to the next level. Look before you leap and enjoy the thrill of flying through the air. Just make sure to tuck in your neck. As with all of your delicate parts, safety is key.

BIRDS OF A FEATHER

COMPATIBLE BIRTHDAY ★ July_27

You are a Snow White among non-animated people. Wildlife are drawn to you because of your deeply good nature. The bluebirds that land on your shoulder are charming. So are the butterflies. It's the scorpions you really have to watch out for.

THE FROGGER

COMPATIBLE BIRTHDAY ★ February_08

Did you ever play the game Frogger? If you did, I bet you were really good at it. If you didn't play, it's time you sought the game out. You've got mad skillz searching for a place to shine. Old Atari games are pretty much your best bet.

THE CONNECT FOUR

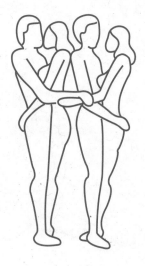

COMPATIBLE BIRTHDAY ★ April_24

Sometimes even though the person you're with is great, you still want someone else. This happens to all of us. The real question is, do you act on these desires? And does your partner know? Polyamory may just be the answer for you.

THE PSYCHIC CONNECTION

COMPATIBLE BIRTHDAY ★ January_22

We all are curious about what the future holds. Where will I live? Who will I marry? Will I have a good job and be famous and rich? You may even consult a psychic to get the answers to some of these questions. This could be a lot of fun. But your energies would be better spent figuring out what you want deep down and making it happen.

OY!

COMPATIBLE BIRTHDAY ★ August_09

You'll occasionally experience times that will make you want to pull your hair out. And then you'll experience other times that will make you want to pull someone else's hair out. And that's okay, as long as they're okay with it. Ask first. Or if you're in the heat of the moment, give their coif a little tug. If they don't tell you to stop or pull away, you're good to go. Yankers away!

THE BORAT

COMPATIBLE BIRTHDAY ★ January_26

It's time for you to make-a the sexy time. Like your cousin Borat, you approach life in a full-bodied kind of way. You have a nice time. And you carry a very special chicken in your suitcase.

MARIA FULL OF GRACE

COMPATIBLE BIRTHDAY ★ February_26

Have you seen the film *Maria Full of Grace*? It's an excellent movie about drug trafficking and immigration. More relevant to you is the movie's title. You would be served well to let grace enter into your life. Maria (or Mario), you too can lead a life full of Grace.

BOBBING FOR APPLES

COMPATIBLE BIRTHDAY ★ October_13

When you bob for apples, the chances of picking one up with your teeth are very slim. So spare your dentifrice and get in there with your hands. You'll find you can pick up the fruits of your labor with great ease. Enjoy your just rewards.

HOLD MY CALLS

COMPATIBLE BIRTHDAY ★ January_07

You know how to work it. You are a dedicated, hardworking employee. Nine to five is just the beginning of it for you. You get in early and stay late, and even schedule business trips during the holidays. You really show a lot of initiative. Or maybe you're just cheating on your spouse.

THE PIÑATA POKE

COMPATIBLE BIRTHDAY ★ October_06

Your life could use a little more fun and festivities. Consider borrowing from the backyard games of yesteryear. Grab a blindfold and a big stick. Poke around for some candy. You'll be surprised to discover what comes out after a few swings.

HOT FOR TEACHER

COMPATIBLE BIRTHDAY ★ October_31

You learned a lot in school—but not as much as you learned once you got out. You've found that there is knowledge all around you and people you can learn from. You get to pick your lessons and what you want to have for homework. And at least now no one will go to jail if you're hot for teacher.

HANG HIM OUT TO DRY

COMPATIBLE BIRTHDAY ★ June_18

You don't want to air your dirty laundry for the world to see. That's why you clean it well before you hang it outside to dry in the sun. This is a good technique, but one that can leave certain items feeling a little rough. Take your delicates to the laundromat to dry instead. Except for stained items—they really ought to be hung out to dry, lest they set permanently.

THE HAMMER AND NAIL-HER

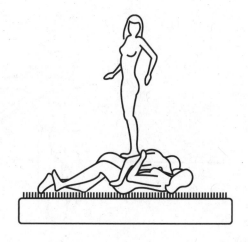

COMPATIBLE BIRTHDAY ★ November_12

The cool thing about a bed of nails is that when you lie on one your weight is supposed to be evenly distributed, so you don't get impaled. Think about life this way. Sometimes it will be full of nails, but if you can distribute yourself across them in an even manner, all will be well. Just don't put extra weight on any one nail or you may risk crucifixion.

ORGASM OR BUST

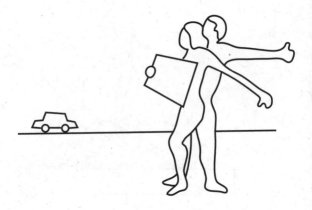

COMPATIBLE BIRTHDAY ★ April_11

Why take a bus when you can rely on the kindness of strangers to get you places? Like many things in life, you just need to put your thumb up and let your intentions be known, and what you seek will pull up right in front of you and get you where you wish to go. Just try not to get picked up by an ax murderer. Then buckle up and enjoy the detours along the way.

THE SECOND STORY LIFT

COMPATIBLE BIRTHDAY ★ May_05

Lately you've been feeling a little behind. It's okay. It happens to the best of us. Keep plugging away at what you're doing and you'll get the job done. At this rate, you'll even get some bonus work done. Somebody's going to be up for a raise!

IT WAS THE BEST OF TIMES, IT WAS THE WORST OF TIMES

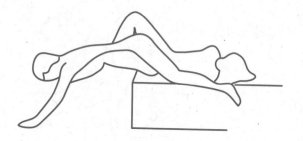

COMPATIBLE BIRTHDAY ★ May_17

You could use a little more support in your relationship. Some of your needs are being met, but there are still some areas where you're being left hanging. Enjoy what's good and try to reposition yourself so you get what you need. If that doesn't work, think about buying a bigger mattress and an eHarmony membership.

"PEEKABOO"

COMPATIBLE BIRTHDAY ★ March_09

Have you lost sight of something important lately? Has something you care about fallen out of view? It's time to take inventory of what's important to you and make an effort to reincorporate the missing pieces back into your world.

SATURDAY IN THE PARK

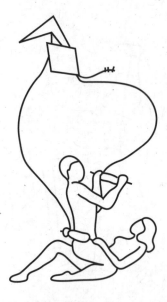

COMPATIBLE BIRTHDAY ★ December_03

There's nothing quite as nice as a Saturday in the park. You could use a little time outdoors. You have a tendency to turn greenish and sickly looking when you're indoors too long. Get yourself an appointment with Dr. Sun.

"OBJECTION, YOUR HONOR"

COMPATIBLE BIRTHDAY ★ December_20

We live in an extremely litigious society. And because it's such a lucrative field, being a lawyer has always appealed to you. But the idea of three years of law school and all those torts and memorization has never settled well with you. You'd sue yourself for putting you through such hardship.

THE RORSCHACH TEST

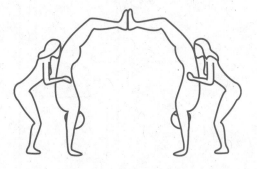

COMPATIBLE BIRTHDAY ★ October_14

Much of life is like a big inkblot. A Rorschach test, if you will. There are a lot of things just sitting there open to our interpretation. What we see in these inanimate things around us can be deeply revealing. How are you revealing yourself?

THE PINBALL WIZARD

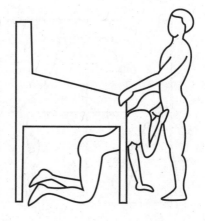

COMPATIBLE BIRTHDAY ★ May_16

Pinball wizardry is a gift you are partially born with and one that is also acquired over time. You were born with many gifts, and should invest in developing your talents into skills that will win you many friends and admirers in bars.

OCTOBER_07

THE PARTED DRAPES

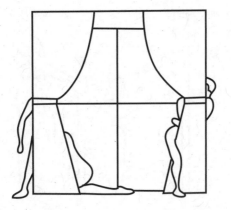

COMPATIBLE BIRTHDAY ★ May_19

You have an eye for interior design and spare no detail when you are creating a unique space. You know that window dressing makes the window. It's also a very pleasant touch when the curtains match the drapes. Keep up the good work and you're sure to attract and satisfy many customers.

THE OLD-FASHIONED SYSTEM SPRINKLER

COMPATIBLE BIRTHDAY ★ July_3

Gardening is a wonderful, centering, beautifying kind of hobby. It's good to get your hands in the dirt and connect with the earth. You could use a hobby of this kind. Get yourself outside and plant a bulb deep into the soil.

THE FARMER'S DAUGHTER

COMPATIBLE BIRTHDAY ★ March_27

Small farms are hard to come by in these times of industrial agriculture. It's no wonder you wanted to buy that farm when you had the chance. But tractors are expensive and dangerous. And you don't want to wake up every morning to milk the cows, do you? Better to just find a nice farmhand or farmer's daughter to take back to your comfortable life in the city.

THE TWIST AND SHOUT

COMPATIBLE BIRTHDAY ★ April_20

While they may result in the occasional complication, your entanglements generally bring you much happiness and satisfaction. It is therefore important for you to stay limber and open in your life. Maintaining a sense of adventure will make you happier than the proverbial clam.

THE DEAD ON ARRIVAL

COMPATIBLE BIRTHDAY ★ September_13

In life, you may fall upon hard times. And then you'll fall upon even harder times. And you'll discover even when you feel like you've hit rock bottom that you can go down even deeper. And it's really not so bad down there after all.

THE FORBIDDEN FRUIT

COMPATIBLE BIRTHDAY ★ July_22

Mankind has known temptation since the dawn of, well, mankind. You've eaten the fruit of the tree of knowledge and man, it was delicious. It really opened your eyes up to a lot of things—like that there's a snake wrapped around you. A little fruit in you can go a long way.

THE BINOCULARS

COMPATIBLE BIRTHDAY ★ October_15

Lately you're having trouble seeing what's right in front of you. Maybe you're not looking at the right things. Try taking a closer look. It's all right there before you. Why postpone the joy of discovery?

THE HUNT FOR RED OCTOBER

COMPATIBLE BIRTHDAY ★ September_21

Sometimes the best way to get at a problem is from underneath it. Like being in a submarine with a periscope looking out for dangerous ships at sea. If you don't find anything's wrong up top, you may just find something that's right, like a two-legged mermaid or merman submerged for your pleasure.

THE JOY OF CHICKEN FIGHTING

COMPATIBLE BIRTHDAY ★ May_06

You've never liked being called a chicken. No one does. Why else would people stack themselves on top of each other just for the chance to defend their non-chicken status and honor? Make sure that you get enough support in your fight to stay on top.

KING ME

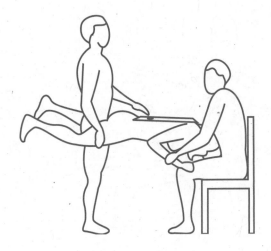

COMPATIBLE BIRTHDAY ★ October_03

You've always enjoyed playing games. They give you a chance to see into the mind of your opponents in ways you never could by just going to dinner or catching a movie. And this time spent learning their strategies also teaches you how you can defeat them in bigger, real-life ways.

THE SHOE SALESMAN

COMPATIBLE BIRTHDAY ★ July_09

New union rules say that salespeople in shoe stores no longer have to help you try on shoes. Remember how they used to slip your foot into the shoe and lace it up and then feel to see where your big toe ended? Well, they don't do that anymore. And this concerns you because you care about a comfortable, well-fitted shoe. Not to worry. If you're a nice customer, you'll be sure to receive good service.

THE SIDE SWIPE

COMPATIBLE BIRTHDAY ★ February_18

Have you ever been sideswiped in your car? Two bodies crashing into each other from the side can cause a great deal of friction— enough to leave a groove and scratch your finish. But not to worry. You were wise enough to get a comprehensive insurance policy.

CHURNING THE MILK

COMPATIBLE BIRTHDAY ★ November_09

As a child, when someone held a buttercup under your chin it was very clear that you liked butter. As you've gotten older you've found that you have more in common with the Land O' Lakes girl than you ever realized. You are both Native American, have nice knees, and occasionally churn butter.

THE NICOTINE FIX

COMPATIBLE BIRTHDAY ★ October_08

Most people wait to have their cigarette after sex. Not you. Your addiction to both sex and cigarettes makes it difficult for you to do one without the other. Something's got to give. Cigarette prices are going up. Sex is free. You do the math.

THE SMURFBERRY CRUNCH

COMPATIBLE BIRTHDAY ★ November_20

You've got your finger in some pretty interesting pies these days. Sample all the filling you want—but be careful to avoid the crust. That's the part that's not as good for you.

THE BREAK JOB

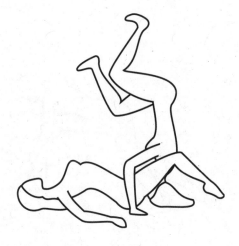

COMPATIBLE BIRTHDAY ★ September_09

With you at the helm, breakdancing could make a big comeback.
You can pop and lock with the best of them. Get out your boom box
and show the world (or at least the people on the subway platform)
what you can do.

THE DEVIL MADE ME DO IT

COMPATIBLE BIRTHDAY ★ September_06

Don't you sometimes just want to strangle the ones you love? That doesn't mean you love them any less. It's just that sometimes life would be so much easier if they weren't breathing. But you know that's not something you're supposed to think. So loosen your grip and let go of some expectations, and things will be A-OK.

THE LOVE POTION

COMPATIBLE BIRTHDAY ★ November_13

You are a scientific person. "Better living through chemistry" is something you take quite seriously. The very fabric of our lives has been altered and improved by science. Where would we be without plastic and all of the fine products that can be made from it? You are convinced that without it you'd have an empty, hollow feeling inside.

THE DIZZY LIZZY

COMPATIBLE BIRTHDAY ★ June_04

Sometimes things feel a little upside-down for you. But that's a good feeling. Who's to say the only way to experience the world is right-side up? There's a lot that you can see when you look at things from a new angle.

THE STAIRWAY TO HEAVEN

COMPATIBLE BIRTHDAY ★ March_05

Someone once tried to insult you by telling you your lip looked like a roller coaster. This is ridiculous. Your lip looks nothing like a roller coaster. But you do kiss like a roller coaster. That's probably why people are always trying to get on, for a different kind of ride.

THE TIRE SCHWING

COMPATIBLE BIRTHDAY ★ November_04

You believe in reusing old things—like turning old tires into swings, old milk cartons into planters, and old tampon applicators into new tampon applicators. Some of your ideas are better than others—but at least you've got the big ideas right. Schwing!

GOOD TIMES ALL AROUND

COMPATIBLE BIRTHDAY ★ August_19

How many men does it take to really love a woman? It's hard to find everything you're looking for in one partner. Keep an open mind and you'll find ways to get everything you need.

ON YOUR MARKS, GET SET, GO

COMPATIBLE BIRTHDAY ★ January_19

There's the old way to do things and there's the new way to do things. The new ways are good. And the old ways are timeless. You'd be well-served to combine the old with the new in all of your endeavors. Embrace new technologies while holding on to what has worked in the past.

THE SPACE INVADER

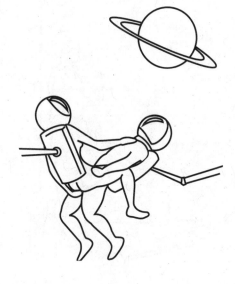

COMPATIBLE BIRTHDAY ★ October_17

Lately you've been feeling a little adrift in your life. Take a deep breath. Things aren't as out there as you think. You'll soon find a cosmic connection. It's in the stars.

OCTOBER_31

THE HARD CANDY

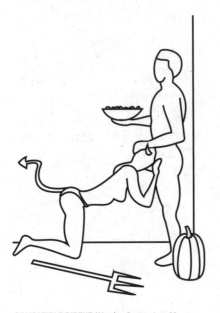

COMPATIBLE BIRTHDAY ★ September_26

You are a child of the night. Born on the day when spirits run free, you've been touched by some particularly wild ones. You embrace all that your day of birth represents—costumes, tricks, and plenty of hard candy.

THE FOOT FETISH

COMPATIBLE BIRTHDAY ★ April_17

You've never been into fetishes. Except for when it comes to feet.
You can't help yourself. All those sexy little toes calling out your
name. That beautiful little heel screaming for attention. That's the
thing about fetishes. You don't choose them, they choose you.

THE MILKMAID

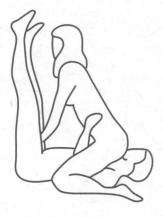

COMPATIBLE BIRTHDAY ★ January_21

Coming from a long line of dairy farmers, you have an innate fondness for cows and all things dairy. Milk—it really does do a body good. Got some?

"ARE YOU SURE I HAVE TO BE HANGING FROM THE CEILING TO DO THIS?"

COMPATIBLE BIRTHDAY ★ October_22

You have a tendency to make things more complicated than they need to be. This is one of your challenges and also one of your charms. You do things that were previously unimagined. You dangle from the ceiling, put butter on your toast before putting it in the toaster, and wear a fedora in the shower. No one ever said being original would be easy.

THE SLEEPER CAR

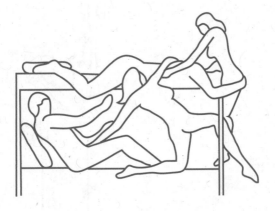

COMPATIBLE BIRTHDAY ★ May_01

Some like it hot, while others like it cold. Some like riding in trains. Others prefer buses. Some like sleeping in bunk beds. Others prefer not sleeping while they're in bunk beds. You are not one of these people. You'll pretty much take anything you can get.

THE TWO-HEADED DRAGON

COMPATIBLE BIRTHDAY ★ June_26

You once bought a house for a song. But that same tactic hasn't bought you love. That's going to cost you. A lot of money. But if you barter well, maybe the object of your affection will give you a deal.

THE PITCHED TENT

COMPATIBLE BIRTHDAY ★ February_07

You know how to pitch a tent. You put the stakes in the ground and use a strong tarp to keep out the rain. This is a really important start. Now if only you knew how to camp.

WHO LET THE DOGS OUT?

COMPATIBLE BIRTHDAY ★ February_11

Who let the dogs out? You. You let the dogs out. And that was just the beginning. Why doesn't anyone ever talk about what happened after that? The story only gets more interesting from there. Why don't you consider letting the story out next? Odds are it could be the basis for another great hit song.

THE WEDDING CRASHERS

COMPATIBLE BIRTHDAY ★ July_13

You have been called "The MFP" (most fun person) at countless parties. You get people singing karaoke and dancing in conga lines, and are the one who starts the official swinging from the chandeliers competitions. A career as a wedding and bar mitzvah DJ would really suit you.

BACK IN THE SADDLE

COMPATIBLE BIRTHDAY ★ March_26

What's been afoot in your life lately, dear Scorpio? You've been a bit of a mystery to those who know you, keeping everyone at bay. But don't worry, fair scorpion. You're building a mystery on the way to a magnificent life.

THE HAPPY HOOKER

COMPATIBLE BIRTHDAY ★ June_27

It's too bad the days of Vaudeville are gone. You really would have been a hit in the Catskills. Regardless, you should take your act on stage. But don't quit your day job just yet. Though Vaudeville is no longer, they still hung on to those Vaudevillian hooks.

THE WHEEL OF FORTUNE

COMPATIBLE BIRTHDAY ★ October_19

Two eyes are typically better than one. The same with eyebrows. But when it comes to bicycles, if you're up for the challenge, a unicycle can be a lot of fun. Be confident and fearless when you ride and you'll have an exhilarating experience.

THE "GENTLEMEN START YOUR ENGINES"

COMPATIBLE BIRTHDAY ★ September_28

You are a pedal-to-the-metal kind of person. You always land the much-coveted pole position. Like a true champion, you rev your engine, raring to go before the race even begins. And when it does, you give it all you've got. Luckily, your helmet helps keep your head on straight in the midst of all those fast turns. Which is a good thing—it makes you realize that there's more to life than just winning. Sometimes it's okay to get lapped.

THE TIPPING POINT

COMPATIBLE BIRTHDAY ★ August_24

You generally manage to create a perfect balance in your life. But sometimes you get thrown, and everything falls apart. This is normal. It happens to even the most well-balanced person—like you. Clean yourself up and get back to where you left off. It's all good.

THE WORKING STIFF

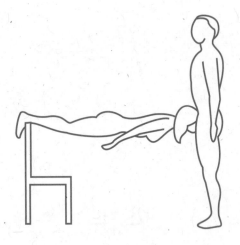

COMPATIBLE BIRTHDAY ★ June_15

Have you ever had one of those séances? The kind where you say repeatedly, "Light as a feather, stiff as a board"? And then you pick someone up with just two fingers? Yeah, that's a pretty cool trick. But it's also some freaky shit. Be careful what you conjure up. You might get more light feathers and stiff boards than you bargained for.

THE FIRST MATE

COMPATIBLE BIRTHDAY ★ January_25

If the old wartime slogan "Loose lips sink ships" is true, you're destined to sink a lot of ships. Your lips are very loose. You talk a lot. But you always have something interesting, witty, charming, or nice to say.

THE TASTE TEST

COMPATIBLE BIRTHDAY ★ September_03

You have great strengths you never even knew you had. You can do anything you set your mind to. Things you never even dreamt were possible are all inside you waiting to happen. So take action. It's time to make some outrageous moves.

THE SADIE HAWKINS

COMPATIBLE BIRTHDAY ★ February_11

You can dance if you want to. But more often than not you would prefer to take things lying down. You still take the lead even when you're doing the horizontal mambo.

"REMIND ME OF YOUR NAME AGAIN"

COMPATIBLE BIRTHDAY ★ April_13

Some things are memorable. And other things are not. Especially when you make it a habit of drinking enough to kill small farmland creatures. Make sure to keep an eye on your consumption—or have a sober buddy close by to make sure you'll have an unforgettable night.

THE BROWNIE POINTS

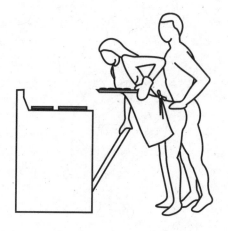

COMPATIBLE BIRTHDAY ★ April_18

Do you often find yourself worrying about a bun you might have in the oven? Well, don't fret. It's a common concern. And one that can be taken care of with a little forethought, good timing, and/or a broken oven.

THE TIE ME UP, TIE ME DOWN

COMPATIBLE BIRTHDAY ★ October_30

When you get home from work at the end of the day, don't just walk in and throw your tie on the floor. Show a little more respect than that. Ties deserve to be treated with care. They had a long day at work too, you know. Why don't you loosen it up and take it out for a bit of fun? You and your tie deserve a good time.

THE BOTTOM FEEDER

COMPATIBLE BIRTHDAY ★ May_27

Your choices determine where you fall on the food chain. You can be at the top, eating steak and lobster. Or you can be happy as a bottom-feeding tofu-eater. There certainly isn't anything wrong with that. The choice is up to you. Bon appétit!

SHRINER'S PARADISE

COMPATIBLE BIRTHDAY ★ August_13

You have a strange feeling lately that you've been dating a dinosaur. While the age gap isn't that great between you, you've noticed that some of your partner's habits are more than old-fashioned—they're outdated. Think about dating someone a little younger and less on the verge of extinction. You don't want people accusing you of trying to rob the grave.

THE FURNITURE OUTLET

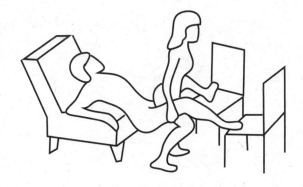

COMPATIBLE BIRTHDAY ★ February_04

You just got a new place to call your own. Somebody's feeling like nesting! And the best way to nest is to go to a vintage furniture store and find some exciting pieces that really suit your personality. Try things out and imagine them in your new home. Then call that man/woman with a van to get your goods on home.

OVER THE RIVER AND THROUGH THE WOODS

COMPATIBLE BIRTHDAY ★ March_20

Participating in a ropes course is a great way to spend time out in nature and build trust with those you hold dear. Nothing says "I trust you" quite like a trust fall, a tire maze, and a zip line. It's time you allowed trust to become less of an obstacle and more a part of the course.

THE URBAN COWBOY

COMPATIBLE BIRTHDAY ★ August_03

With the bucking bronco of your existence, you grab the bull by the horns and ride that mechanical beast until the cows come home. Ain't nothing gonna throw you from the ride of your life (except for maybe a handsome mechanical toreador or other mechanical hottie).

DOROTHY AND THE SCARECROW

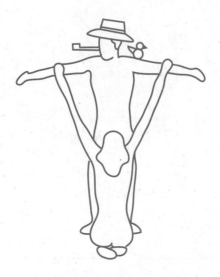

COMPATIBLE BIRTHDAY ★ July_19

Given the choice of having a partner who needs a heart, one who needs brains, one who needs courage, and another who just needs to get home, you'll choose the one in search of brains. You reason that even if they never get any brains, in the end they'll still make a decent mate. If that turns out wrong, just click your heels together and get the hell out of there.

STUFFING THE TURKEY

COMPATIBLE BIRTHDAY ★ March_07

You're a good pilgrim—you want to learn from the natives. Even though you've had a good education and received a sizable inheritance, you still know that people who are different from you have a lot to offer. It's good that you are open to this experience. You'll get a lot out of it, including some really delicious stuffing.

THE HARPOONANI

COMPATIBLE BIRTHDAY ★ January_28

When the ground is shifting beneath you, you might want to try spending some time underwater. A little immersive experience could be just what you need to get your sea legs and better footing on land. You'll also meet sea creatures that will make you happy to be the land-loving person you are.

THE RANCH DRESSING

COMPATIBLE BIRTHDAY ★ November_10

Lately you've been on the fence about something. You can't decide which side you want to be on. It's time to make up your mind one way or the other. No matter what you decide, the grass will still seem greener on the other side. That's just human nature.

THE BAGGAGE CLAIM

COMPATIBLE BIRTHDAY ★ April_01

You don't like waiting for things. You've got places to go. People to, well, see. But sometimes wait you must. Claim the moment. Make it yours. Whether you're in line or waiting for your luggage, hang tight and soon that old bag will be back in your arms.

THE HOT SPOT

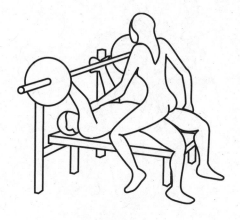

COMPATIBLE BIRTHDAY ★ August_17

You've been spending a lot of time at the gym lately. Isn't it nice
how you can shape your body into new forms with a little effort?
You are so full of shape and tone that others either hate you or
want to love you.

THE CONSTANT GARDENER

COMPATIBLE BIRTHDAY ★ April_12

You are a very attentive gardener. You repot your plants regularly and always fertilize and water them. And you take it a step further than just talking to your little green friends. They help clean your air, and you feel the best way to thank them is to share with them a bit more of who you are.

THE BOB BARKER

COMPATIBLE BIRTHDAY ★ November_03

Come on down! You're the next contestant. And the games you're playing are no challenge for you. Luck, the audience, and the game show host are on your side.

WALKING THE DOG

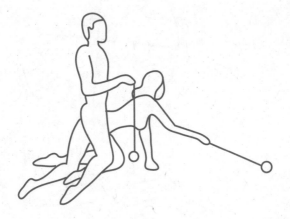

COMPATIBLE BIRTHDAY ★ February_19

You take pleasure in the iconic playthings of your youth. You could go around the world in search of pleasing things, but nothing brings you quite as much joy as staying at home with an old-fashioned yo-yo and walking the dog.

THE DUST BUSTER

COMPATIBLE BIRTHDAY ★ July_12

Fresh out of new ideas? Don't let yourself relax into your safe, old routines. If you have a partner, they can help you come up with something new. If not, the world around you can be your inspiration. Your muse is calling. And she wants to talk to you.

THE WATER FOUNTAIN

COMPATIBLE BIRTHDAY ★ February_03

You think about things in a more critical and slightly more neurotic wa
than most people. For example, you've never felt comfortable drinkin
from public water fountains. Lord only knows what diseases you coul
pick up there. Since you're also not a fan of the wastefulness of drinki
bottled water, you have had to seek out other sources to quench your
neurotic thirst.

HANG GLIDING

COMPATIBLE BIRTHDAY ★ May_20

You're a risk taker. You have big dreams and you pursue them, which has helped you reach great heights. Lately you've been floating in on only a wing and a prayer. Just keep on gliding through the turbulence and enjoy the sights along the way.

DECEMBER_08

THE GOOD RECEPTION

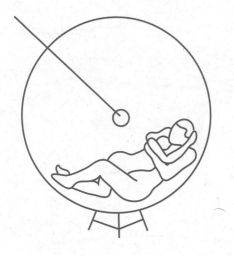

COMPATIBLE BIRTHDAY ★ April_22

Your gracious nature and appetite for variety are greatly appreciated by those around you. You like to give everybody a warm reception, and every party you throw tends to finish with a big bang.

THE SHUTTER BUGGER

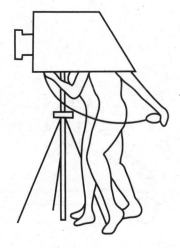

COMPATIBLE BIRTHDAY ★ November_26

You look at the world through a unique lens. You have a distinct perspective and an eye for beauty. Avoid saying "cheese" and press the shutter already. The world is ready for you to capture it.

THE HO-BOS

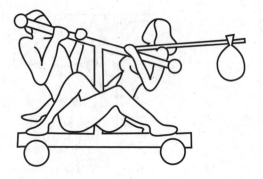

COMPATIBLE BIRTHDAY ★ January_27

You are a resident of the world. All you need you have right there on your back. Take comfort in this. You can make the world your home.

SATURDAY NIGHT BEAVER

COMPATIBLE BIRTHDAY ★ January_02

You can try to understand. And you can try to be a man. But sometimes it's hard to do all of these things when you're quite occupied with staying alive. *Ah ah ah ah . . .*

THE PORTRAIT OF DESIRE

COMPATIBLE BIRTHDAY ★ November_29

All great painters start off doing nudes or figure drawings. Mastering the human form is an important process for an artist. You are not an artist. You just pretend to be one so you can get into one of those life-drawing classes. And that's okay, as long as you pay to get in and at least occasionally touch your brush to the canvas as an artful gesture.

THE SNOWPLOW

COMPATIBLE BIRTHDAY ★ May_04

You haven't found the person that you're looking for yet. Lately that sad reality has been making you feel pretty cold. Don't let this feeling snowball. Take matters into your own hands. Create the one you want to be with—even if you have to settle for a carrot nose.

THE HOLIDAY GIFT

COMPATIBLE BIRTHDAY ★ February_16

You are a very generous person. And though they say it's the thought that counts, you know it's really the wrapping that impresses people the most.

THE ALIEN INVASION

COMPATIBLE BIRTHDAY ★ May_26

Do you really think we're the only planet that has life on it? Of course you do. That's what they've programmed you to think. If they didn't do that, how else would you deal with your weekly appointments with their team of scientists and doctors?

THE PAGE SIX

COMPATIBLE BIRTHDAY ★ April_07

The key to a good life is to learn how to live well and then go ahead and live well. You know where to look to find good models for good living. You'll unlock the secrets to your own happiness—or get arrested for being a Peeping Tom.

THE LUMBERJACK HOLIDAY PARTY

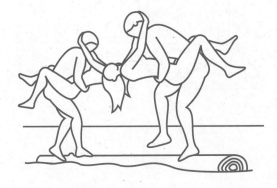

COMPATIBLE BIRTHDAY ★ September_02

Paul Bunyan was your hero as a child. You've always dreamt of cutting down virgin trees and getting some good wood. As long as your interest in lumberjacking doesn't splinter, you'll soon find others who share your dreams.

"COULD YOU GIVE ME A PUSH?"

COMPATIBLE BIRTHDAY ★ January_23

Sometimes you like being pushed around. A little shove really gets you going. Now, that's not to say that you condone violence of any kind. You just happen to like a little roughie-toughie on your rumpy pumpy.

THE BROKEN BONE

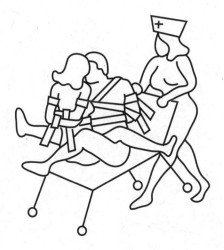

COMPATIBLE BIRTHDAY ★ June_29

Been feeling a bit infirm lately? Is something broken? Could it be your heart? You and yours need professional help. There's nothing wrong with asking for assistance when you need it. And oh boy, do you ever need it.

THE TUMBLEWEED

COMPATIBLE BIRTHDAY ★ February_27

Like a tumbleweed, you come rolling into people's lives, only to roll right out shortly thereafter. You can't stay in one place for too long. You go where the wind blows. And as far as you're concerned, you get blown a lot.

SOME LIKE IT COLD

COMPATIBLE BIRTHDAY ★ March_25

You are a child of winter and you take pleasure in all of its spoils.
You love to bundle up and go outside for a good time. Sleighs,
sleds, skis, skates, snowboards—you have them all. You also have
a really wicked case of frostbite on your genitals.

DECEMBER_22

THE DOORWAY TO HEAVEN

COMPATIBLE BIRTHDAY ★ September_01

You are the kind of person who is always there to help a friend in a jam. You've got your foot in all the right doors and generously share that with those you come into contact with. For you, when one door closes, several others open. You just have to choose which one you want to enter first.

THE "HEEEELP!"

COMPATIBLE BIRTHDAY ★ February_29

A medical maverick, you have saved lives with your patented reverse Heimlich. It dislodges while it delights—leaving those in your care happy and healthy. (Though you should never be allowed to drive an ambulance or other emergency vehicle, as you've been known to also do that in reverse.)

"NAPTIME!"

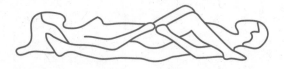

COMPATIBLE BIRTHDAY ★ March_03

Contrary to popular belief, napping is not a sign of laziness. Naps are a time to recharge and reboot your frazzled little mind and body. Benjamin Franklin used to take naps all the time. It's when he had some of his brightest ideas. So give yourself an idea-generating break. Take a five-minute nap once a day!

"AND WHAT DO YOU WANT FOR CHRISTMAS?"

COMPATIBLE BIRTHDAY ★ March_19

Some people may say you look like an elf or a leprechaun, but your lucky charms by far make up for your looks. To the happy surprise of all who truly get to know you, you are magically delicious.

DECEMBER_26

THE JOAN OF ARCH

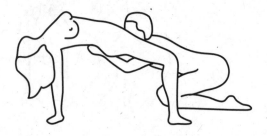

COMPATIBLE BIRTHDAY ★ July_30

Even though you sometimes find yourself bending over backward to help others, you have found that you can receive some nice benefits in return. Continue to give of yourself, and others will not only lap it up, they'll support you where you need it most.

CROSSING THE LINE

COMPATIBLE BIRTHDAY ★ April_19

Eating too much at dinnertime is never pleasant for anyone—unless you do it with someone who shares your appreciation of food and excess. Gluttony loves company!

SHOULDERING THE BURDEN

COMPATIBLE BIRTHDAY ★ May_09

You always get a leg up in life, sometimes two. This serves you well as an accomplished bicyclist, equestrian, or tight-rope walker. When wearing a skirt, you are frequently met with the greeting, "Nice stems."

THE NIGHT CRAWLER

COMPATIBLE BIRTHDAY ★ February_05

Worry not. You shall find the thing you seek—whether it be a lost contact lens, a new career, or a diamond tennis bracelet. Luck is not on your side, it's actually somewhere just behind you—which, as you'll discover, is a very nice place for it to be.

FULL SERVICE

COMPATIBLE BIRTHDAY ★ April_29

With the rising price of gas, it's a wonder anyone can afford to drive.
You drive for pleasure and want to keep that pleasure at any cost.
Consider investing in a hybrid vehicle. Lexus even has a hybrid SUV,
if you like your ride to be big and fast.

THE STROKE OF MIDNIGHT

COMPATIBLE BIRTHDAY ★ February_22

A three-ring circus is entertaining, but a one-man show can be even more impressive. Occasionally suffering from stage fright, you still manage to bring your many talents to the fore. Always remember to keep your costume and makeup at hand, because you never know when you'll be called on to perform. Life, after all, is not a dress rehearsal.

NERVE.COM

Nerve.com is the only intelligent magazine about sex and culture for women and men. Since 1997, Nerve has been publishing provocative essays, stimulating reporting, and sidesplitting commentary on a daily basis, as well as striking photographs of naked people that capture more than just their flesh. Described by *Entertainment Weekly* as *"Playboy's* body with the *New Yorker's* brain," Nerve has won numerous awards, including National Magazine Award nominations, multiple Webby Awards, and a *Forbes* "Best of the Web" selection. In recent years, Nerve has grown into a successful multimedia company, expanding into film, television, books, print, and online personals.